CARING
through the
FUNERAL

Also by Gene Fowler,
published by Chalice Press

The Pastoral Care Case: Learning about Care in Congregations
with Donald Capps

CARING
through the
FUNERAL

A Pastor's Guide

GENE FOWLER

CHALICE
PRESS
ST. LOUIS, MISSOURI

Cover art: Artville, LLC
Cover design: Elizabeth Wright
Interior design: Hui-chu Wang
Art direction: Elizabeth Wright

This book is printed on acid-free, recycled paper.

Visit Chalice Press on the World Wide Web at
www.chalicepress.com

10 9 8 7 6 5 4 3 2 1   04 05 06 07 08 09

Library of Congress Cataloging–in–Publication Data
Fowler, Gene, 1952-
  Caring through the funeral / Gene Fowler.
    p. cm.
Includes bibliographical references and index.
  ISBN 0-8272-0493-0 (pbk. : alk. paper)
  1. Pastoral theology. 2. Funeral service. I. Title.
BV4330.F69 2004
265'.85–dc22
                                    2003026536

Printed in the United States of America

Contents

*This book is dedicated to
all who mourn in the post-9/11 world.*

Acknowledgments

I want to thank my wife and son for their support while I was writing this book, and for their unending patience. I also want to thank every caring pastor who shared a funeral story with me. Few people realize how courageous ministers are as they face emotionally difficult situations involving death and bereavement time after time. Next, I want to acknowledge pastoral theologian Paul Irion for his mid-twentieth century books on funerals. I believe that his works on funerals are among the finest pastoral care books written during the mid-twentieth century. Finally, I want to thank my editor during the writing of this book, Jon Berquist, for his help and support, and for his astute awareness of the topic about which this book is written.

Introduction

If you search for books on funerals at popular bookstores, or even in a good theological library, you will find very few choices. Although there is a mountain of literature on grief, books focusing primarily on funerals are few and far between. Ministers, however, need literature on funerals, because conducting funerals requires learning many things, such as how grief and funerals are related. The main thesis that will unfold in this book is that the funeral is a ministry of caring for the bereaved.

The funeral is a massive subject. For instance, funerals in all religions share the common bond of being funerals, yet each one contains its own rites, which could provide a fruitful focus for interreligious dialogue. In this book, the focus is squarely on funerals in Protestant Christianity, though attention is given to their commonality with all funerals. Within Christianity, funerals can be approached from the standpoint of any theological discipline, such as church history or biblical studies. I am writing as a pastoral theologian, and as a pastor whose ministry is in the congregational setting. My focus will be on the ministry of funerals seen from the standpoint of pastoral care.

Within pastoral care, there still is room for a variety of emphases, such as writing for church members who have lost a loved one, or for clergy. This book is for pastors who conduct funerals, first and foremost. However, I believe that lay church leaders and others also can read this book fruitfully. Among the others I have in mind are psychotherapists and psychiatrists who work with bereaved people and who want to learn more about the relationship between funerals and the grief process.

Notice that so far I have used the terms *clergy, ministers,* and *pastors.* In my first church, I often went by the name preacher. In another church I served, I was called pastor, and some believed it was disrespectful to use my given name, Gene. In my present church, however, normally I am called by my given name. Yet, if a church member introduces me to someone, I will be called the minister, as in "This is our minister, Gene Fowler." Or, in such a situation, I also may be called Rev. Fowler, or once in a while Dr. Fowler. It seems that, whatever my official title or position, the name by which normally I am addressed in the congregation depends on the tradition of the particular church I am serving within my denomination, which is the Presbyterian Church (USA).

1

The terminology used for identifying clergy who practice pastoral care has become a significant issue. On the one hand, there needs to be terminology that is inclusive, embracing clergy in whatever setting they work, whether it is teaching, administration, chaplaincy, campus ministry, pastoral psychotherapy, or the congregation. On the other hand, there needs to be terminology differentiating between the settings and types of ministry that go with them. For instance, pastor, chaplain and pastoral psychotherapist have been used to identify those who work in a church, an institution such as a medical center and a pastoral counseling center. While the terminological issues may be resolved at some future point, in the meantime I imagine I will continue being addressed by different names in congregations. So, here is how the ministry terminology will be used in this book. First, I will be using the term *clergy* very little, though it seems to be the most inclusive term for ordained ministry. Second, I mostly will be using the terms *minister* and *pastor* more or less interchangeably, and in some cases I will use *reverend*, as in Rev. Fowler. Because those in pastoral ministry can be called by so many names, the book reflects this ambiguity, though the term *minister* can be, and often should be, used appropriately as a more inclusive term than *pastor* (see Capps, 2001, 5).

The reason I am addressing ordained ministry in the congregational setting is because those in pastoral ministry are on the front lines dealing with funerals. However, those in specialized ministries are included in the discussion implicitly, because they too must deal with the main issues being addressed when they conduct funerals. For instance, the first phase of grief, and the mourning process accompanying it, is discussed extensively, which has relevance for ministers conducting funerals, regardless of the setting in which they work. In addition, those in pastoral ministry and in specialized ministry may conduct funerals for families who have no church.

At the same time, being explicit about the ministry setting makes it more possible to discern differences between the settings, which also may have relevance for conducting funerals. For example, the minister of a church, who may conduct the funeral of a church member in the sanctuary, is part of an interwoven church community and often has an ongoing relationship with the bereaved family. In addition, the minister has to deal with other bereaved individuals and groups within the church over time. Those in specialized ministry who conduct a funeral are more likely to be dealing with the bereaved family, and perhaps close friends, for a limited period, and will not have to deal with an ongoing church community. This difference alone can result in very different choices for the funeral liturgy, as well as affect the location of the funeral. I will not attempt to point out similarities and differences between the settings with regard to funerals. However, I invite those in specialized ministries to identify such differences, as well as similarities, according to their own experience in the service of growing in the ministry of funerals.

There are several important boundaries in this book. The first one has to do with grief, specifically the ways different people experience grief. Some differences are based on gender, and others are based on age. Moreover, we can add any number of similarities and differences, such as those having to do with society, culture, race, ethnicity, and religious tradition. These have implications for conducting funerals, depending on the mourners participating. However, charting and comparing such differences will not be the focus of the book.

The second boundary is that the book stops a few weeks after the funeral. Focusing on caring for the bereaved through the entire grief process is a second book. It is a more complex and long-lasting ministry than pastoral care and counseling has portrayed in the past, and it deserves far more attention than it has yet received, especially in the congregational setting.

The third boundary is that lay care of the bereaved is not in focus. Nevertheless, when I discuss pastoral care practiced by the minister with bereaved church members, I am doing so with the awareness that such care exists as part of a much larger caring network in congregations. I will point toward lay care from time to time in the book.

By the same token, not nearly enough attention has been paid to the very beginnings of grief and mourning, or to the funeral itself. The beginning of grieving and the ritual ways that human beings address it are exceedingly important for the future health of bereaved individuals, families, churches, communities, and sometimes even nations. Those in pastoral ministry play a far more critical role in this than has been acknowledged, so a focus on pastoral ministry and funerals is sorely needed.

Along with the focus on funerals, I have incorporated numerous cases about actual pastoral ministry before and during funerals. Some of these cases are mine, and some are those of other pastors who have been kind enough to share with me what I have come to call their funeral stories. In each and every instance, I have taken care to disguise the cases by changing names, places, times, and sometimes gender. I consider them to be a vital part of the book, because there are hardly any such cases on funerals to be found in the pastoral care and counseling literature during the last half century.

In chapter 1, I will introduce the subject of funerals by presenting an overview of what happens, beginning when the pastor is informed of a death and is asked to officiate at the funeral, going through the time leading up to the funeral, and concluding with the funeral itself. This time includes many familiar things, but it also includes surprises that keep it from becoming routine.

In chapter 2, I will introduce what I have called the language of loss. This is the vocabulary ministers need for their caring ministry of funerals, including bereavement, loss, grief, and mourning. An important part of this discussion is the introduction of grief and mourning processes. Even more important, however, is understanding the distinction between grief and mourning, which is essential for understanding care through funerals.

Chapter 3 moves from a broad overview of bereavement to a focus on the very beginning of grief. This focus is important for pastors and others who deal with bereaved people before and during funerals. The first part of grief begins when a person discovers the death, and it continues at least through the time of the funeral. I also will discuss some of the variables making grief unique for different people during this time.

Chapter 4 shifts to an explicit focus on pastoral care prior to the funeral in pastoral ministry, with some mention of funerals. This is when the minister deals with bereaved family members and friends in preparation for the funeral. Several cases about pastoral care with family members before and during funerals are included.

Chapter 5 is a continuation of chapter 4. It expands from a focus on caring for bereaved family members to those beyond the family. These are non-family individuals and groups who also grieve the loss of the deceased. This chapter contains cases about caring for bereaved groups in the church, and it contains discussion and cases about traumatized churches and communities, when there is a death whose impact reaches far beyond the immediate family and friends.

In chapter 6, I will define and discuss the funeral, primarily the Protestant Christian funeral understood theologically. In the second half of the chapter, I will begin comparing four different liturgical books, each associated with a different denomination. The purpose of this comparison is to provide instructions for helping worship leaders prepare funerals.

Chapter 7 is a continuation of chapter 6. In this chapter, I will continue the comparison in order to unfold all the liturgical elements comprising the Christian funeral, or all its main parts. In most books on funerals, the main emphasis is on preaching. However, in actual pastoral ministry, attention must be given to the entire funeral liturgy. This is important for two reasons. The minister has to know how to prepare the entire liturgy, and it is the entire liturgy, not just preaching, that is important for caring through funerals.

Chapter 8 is the lynchpin chapter holding the entire book together. I will focus on mourning seen in relationship to funerals in order to explain how funerals can be viewed as a form of caring for the bereaved. The funeral will be discussed as a rite of passage, and the interrelationship among funerals, mourning, and grief will be explored.

Chapter 9 builds on the previous chapter. I will discuss the way the worship leader, the pastor, helps bring about caring for the mourners who attend the funeral. I will argue that pastors must embark on a spiritual journey in which they encounter grief, death, and hope in order to practice the caring ministry of funerals effectively. These three spiritual issues will be addressed in relation to funerals and pastoral care.

In chapter 10, I will discuss the most desirable result of caring through funerals, which is comforting the mourners. Comfort is desirable, because it is more than just bringing temporary relief from the pain of grief. Rather, it can help prepare mourners for what lies ahead during the weeks and months after the funeral. It must be sought with humility, however, because there is no guarantee that a funeral will bring comfort, especially when all the mourners are considered.

In the final chapter, chapter 11, I will discuss the first post-funeral pastoral care encounters between the bereaved, the pastor, and the congregation. These are viewed as certain kinds of post-funeral rites having significant consequences for long-term pastoral care of church members. This discussion includes an introduction to the middle phase of grief and the mourning processes accompanying it. There also is a section on the self-care of ministers who officiate at funerals, with special attention given to those who conduct funerals on a regular basis. The chapter concludes with some suggestions for understanding pastoral care throughout the grief process.

In a brief postscript, I will make an observation about grief at the societal level. We live in a world traumatized by war, shown on television. Continuing violence witnessed around the world has a profoundly negative effect on the ability of contemporary societies to grieve and heal.

Finally, I want to express a word of caution. Writing about bereavement is humbling, because bereavement can include extremely powerful emotions and massive life changes. In describing these experiences, or discussing them in terms of psychological models, any author runs the risk of missing the profound impact that bereavement may be having on those who are going through it. Although discussing funerals requires writing about bereavement in spite of this risk, my caution is to keep in mind that the experience of bereavement, as well as the experience of going through a funeral as a pastor or as a mourner, cannot be contained fully in these pages. This being said, I also believe that the descriptions, models, and funeral stories included in the book do convey substantial meaning that can be helpful to new and experienced ministers in their effort to care for the bereaved through funerals.

CHAPTER ONE

From Ordinary Time to Funeral Time

Have you ever stood in line waiting to ride a roller coaster, and when you finally take off you have a wild ride? When you are asked to do a funeral, it can be like finding yourself on a roller coaster without having had the benefit of waiting in line so that you can prepare yourself. One minute it's an ordinary week, and the next minute your entire schedule has been put hold as you enter a process that will not end until after the funeral days later. You, the pastor, have made what could be called a transition from ordinary time to funeral time, a very fast-paced few days filled with phone calls, conversations, and worship planning.

One significant characteristic of funeral time is that there are certain things a minister does routinely, such as visiting with the loved ones of the deceased and attending the visitation, or viewing, before the funeral. These events give funeral time a certain stability in the sense that a very similar series of events tends to happen with each new death and funeral. In this chapter, I will discuss some of these very common events that characterize funeral time. But there is a corresponding characteristic that challenges the stability of these events. This challenge comes from the variety of circumstances that you may encounter all along the way, which can infuse this time with unfamiliarity and, consequently, uncertainty about how to respond. This variety, too, will be discussed within the context of the events characterizing funeral time.

Being Informed of a Death

There are several ways for a minister to find out that someone has died. The telephone is the most common way, when a family member, friend, or the funeral home calls to let you know about the death. Another way happens when you are visiting the hospital, and the death has occurred before you arrive or occurs while you are there, but this is far less common. I wouldn't mention these obvious things, except that the challenging variety starts here.

Let's say, for instance, that you are in your office when you receive a phone call from a church member. George, in obvious distress, tells you that his wife, Joan, has just died in a car accident. Can you feel the roller coaster starting up that first scary hill? You have to deal with your own shock at hearing the news and at the same time manage to respond in a caring way as the pastor of the church. Perhaps the last thing you end up saying is, "Where are you now?...I'll be right there." The rest of that day, along with the days that follow, turn out radically different than you had planned. Contrast this with a situation in which a church member, Martin, has been lingering near death for several weeks and finally has died after a long terminal illness. One of his two adult children, the one who lives in town but is not a member of your congregation, calls you at 7 p.m. to tell you about the death. This is not unexpected, and you are spared a sense of trauma. You will be receiving a phone call from the funeral home the next morning to confirm funeral plans, but you won't be seeing any family members until the other adult child arrives from out of town. Your schedule will be revised over the next few days, but there will be no radical changes.

Your reaction to the news of death, your response to the bearer of that sad news, and your pastoral actions that follow depend on the circumstances associated with the death, which indicates that there is no one right way to handle the situation, but instead that you must try to use good judgment appropriate to the circumstances. This gives you a certain amount of freedom in your responses.

The Minister's Response to Death

A number of years ago, I was in the second month of pastoring a new church when I noticed that a woman who was not a church member started attending worship on Sundays. I soon found out that she was married to a church member I had not met or even heard of at that point. He was in his early eighties, and she was in her early seventies. This was a second marriage for each of them, their previous spouses having been dead for several years. He had been suffering with cancer for two years and was considered terminal at this point. I began visiting him in his home once a week for a half hour or so, and this continued for five months. He was quite a talker, and I mostly listened. I discovered he had two daughters and was estranged from one of them. She would not visit and would have nothing to do with his present wife, which troubled them greatly. I also learned something I have encountered several times since. After the medical establishment pronounced his illness terminal, he began reading about alternative cures, such as pills developed from certain parts of the shark's body and various exotic-sounding treatments found in places such as South America. I never have had the experience of seeing any alternative treatments for cancer save anyone's life, and they did not save his.

It was June. My family and I had been invited by friends to spend a week on a beautiful island five miles out from the mainland in the Gulf of Mexico. This was very special for us, and we really were looking forward to it. Three weeks before we were scheduled to leave, I told him that I would not be visiting during my vacation week because I would be out of town. His immediate response took me completely by surprise as he said, "Then who will bury me?" It wasn't "I hope I don't die while you're gone" or "What contingency plans can we make in case I die while you are gone?" No, it was a flat-out statement implying that he was going to die that week, complete with the fear of my not being there to do the funeral. I felt like a deer caught in the headlights. Most times his wife did not participate in our conversations, but she was present for this one. We looked at each other, and then I responded that I would return for the funeral if he died while I was gone, which seemed to put him at ease. Sure enough, he died toward the end of my vacation week, causing my family and me to return two days early so that I could conduct the funeral.

On the one hand, I felt sorrow that someone I had come to know over half a year was gone. On the other hand, I was irritated at missing the last two days of that very special vacation, not to mention feeling guilty over causing my family to miss those two days. Now before you go calling me a selfish so-and-so, let me explain. What I really was upset about was having allowed myself to be manipulated into promising to return for the funeral during the vacation if he died. Had he not said what he did, and, instead, had I volunteered to return because I felt it to be my pastoral responsibility, I would have maintained a sense of control over my life. As it was, I had lost a sense of control, which did not feel very good. Undoubtedly, my mixed feelings must have had some impact on my preparation for the funeral and my participation in it, but I did not have time to reflect on my responses until later.

Although this situation may invite evaluation in greater depth, the point is that pastors have emotional responses when people in their churches die. In turn, these responses may influence the pastor's interaction with bereaved family members and friends, choices the pastor makes in funeral preparation, and the pastor's worship leadership in the funeral itself.

One significant factor in a minister's emotional reaction to the impending death of a church member, and to the death itself, is the minister's own personal and family history. For example, I can ask myself how I could have visited a terminally ill cancer patient for five months without either one of us ever addressing the funeral. Moreover, why did

I not recover from his surprising statement, made in response to news of my vacation, so that I could clarify what he meant? In order to answer these questions, I also can ask myself whether there was something from my life influencing my reactions to him. In order to find out, I took some time for quiet reflection. Almost immediately, I remembered someone in my family who had died several years earlier. I had just begun graduate school when I received a phone call from my father telling me that my grandmother, his mother, had died. I chose not to return home for the funeral for what seemed like legitimate reasons at the time. I couldn't afford the flight, I was just starting a graduate program, and I was having what undoubtedly were stress-related muscle spasms in my lower back, which would have made a plane ride difficult. It may be, then, that years later I was paying the price of not having dealt with my grandmother's death and funeral. Perhaps it is psychological justice that what he said to me, which startled me so much, must have echoed a voice from deep within me that I did not want to hear, a voice saying I should have attended my grandmother's funeral. Perhaps dealing with the funeral of the terminally ill man would have caused me to be confronted with my guilt over not attending her funeral and with my grief over her death.

Another factor helping to determine a minister's emotional reaction to the death of a church member is the nature of the relationship that the pastor had with the person before the death. Did the person become a close friend of yours over ten years? Then surely you will be far more personally upset than if you had known the person only a short time, especially if the two of you remained like strangers and never became emotionally connected.

A third factor is the age of the person. People can die at any age, whether they are infants, children, teenagers, young adults, middle-aged adults, or older adults. Do you respond emotionally to the death of a seven-year-old in exactly the same way as the death of someone who is ninety-five? How are you likely to react to the death of a middle-aged adult supporting a large family as opposed to the death of a single young adult?

A fourth factor involves the circumstances preceding the death. This may include the pastor's involvement with the person during a protracted illness, for instance, as opposed to a sudden and unexpected death. A homebound woman was cared for by her husband of forty years. She had suffered a debilitating stroke that impaired her speech and partially paralyzed her. The pastor, who had begun serving her church after she had the stroke, brought communion to her at home several times a year for two years. Then, she had more strokes and died. Though it was a great loss to her husband, he was the first to say some words that become familiar to pastors over time: "Pastor, her death was a blessing." The pastor had seen the suffering and knew what the husband meant.

Though the pastor never had the opportunity to know the woman in earlier, pre-stroke years, experiencing her in those final two years gave the pastor an appreciation of her courage in daily living.

Actually, the pastor had a stronger emotional response to the grief of the devoted husband than to the death of his wife. This relates to a fifth factor affecting the minister's emotional response to the death of a church member. In many cases, the minister, along with church members and other acquaintances of the one who dies, may have powerful emotional reactions to the family members and close friends who lose a dearly loved person to death. One of my most difficult moments was standing in a hospital hallway with a mother and her son as she told him that his father was not going to make it. Grief in which the death is anticipated, and grief after the death occurs, too often has been portrayed as if it belongs only to one person, the family member closest to the deceased, and as if it does not go hand-in-hand with feelings for family members suffering the loss. But pastoral ministry shatters that view. The emotional reactions of the minister and others, in response to the impending death and death of a church member, are of a piece with emotional reactions to the loving family members and very close friends of the one who is near death or who has just died.

Being Asked to Conduct the Funeral

Being informed of a death is not the same thing as being asked to conduct the funeral. Many times, perhaps most times, the two come together in the same conversation, but not always. Perhaps the family is assuming that you will do the funeral, but they are in shock and no one has thought to mention it yet. If you are wondering, then don't be afraid to ask if it seems appropriate at the time.

When you receive a phone call from the funeral home and both find out about the death and are asked to do the funeral, be sensitive to the likelihood of the family sitting in the funeral director's office. If you are wondering about their presence, this is another time to ask.

If the deceased was a church member, or if the family members are church members, then your responsibility to do the funeral is clear. You may have some input regarding day and time of the funeral, depending on circumstances, and you can be helpful. For instance, in one city where I lived, a funeral is typically followed by a meal at a local restaurant. If the funeral can be in the late morning rather than in the middle of the afternoon, the mourners will not have to suffer through as long a wait for the funeral to begin, and the meal will happen at an appropriate and helpful time. If you have the opportunity to set indecision to rest, suggest the most strategic time for the funeral.

Customarily, remuneration, about which the funeral director may inquire in the phone conversation, may be set aside when the funeral is for a church member, but even this is not cut and dried. The family often will give you a financial gift at the time of the funeral. Or, depending on the policy of the funeral home, it may be included in the cost of the funeral, and the funeral home will give the pastor a check instead of the family. Be gracious and flexible.

If you are like most pastors, occasionally you will receive funeral home calls in which you are asked to do the funeral of a stranger whose family has no church, or no minister, or who may be coming from out of town. It is up to you to accept or turn down these requests unless your church has a written policy addressing this issue. Ordinarily, the minister receives remuneration when the funeral is for non–church members. One minister suggests you can avoid troublesome situations by clarifying the church's policy regarding the minister's remuneration for funerals when you are negotiating a call or soon after you begin working at your church (Mansell, 1998, 38).

There are times when a church member who dies will have had no family in your congregation. In this case, relatives who have no church, are from out of town, or belong to another church most often will ask you to do the funeral, but not always. Once in a great while you may find that relatives want their own pastor to do the funeral, in which case the funeral would be at their church or at the funeral home, but not at your church. Perhaps you will be asked to participate by reading scripture or saying a prayer.

On other occasions, when you are the one doing the funeral, the family may request that a former pastor, who may have been idealized over the years, participate in the funeral. Although you are the worship leader in the funeral, the other pastor will participate in some way. In that situation, it is up to you to take the initiative and figure out what specific thing you want the other pastor to do in the funeral, such as praying, or you can make suggestions while being open to suggestions from the other pastor. Typically, details between you and the other minister can be worked out in a phone conversation, though family requests in this regard must be taken into account. Again, be gracious and flexible. Your ego should not be on the line here. However, in your church, and in a funeral for your church member, you are the one who takes leadership. Like most other things relating to funerals, the customary patterns of more than one minister participating in a funeral may vary greatly from one region of the country to another.

There are also clergy ethics regarding the appropriate involvement of a former pastor or other pastor in a funeral in which the deceased was a church member of the present pastor. For instance, two pastors had gotten to know each other casually through participation in their young children's sports teams. One of these two pastors had a death in the church and was asked to conduct the funeral, but because some family members belonged to the other pastor's church, which was in a different denomination, that pastor was asked to participate. The funeral was going according to plan. The pastor who was leading the service had just finished the sermon, which was twelve minutes long, when the second pastor stood up, supposedly to speak briefly. Instead, this pastor preached for twenty minutes in a style that was unappreciated by most of the church members present, including family members who were not part of that pastor's congregation. Naturally, this left the other pastor and the church members, including most of the family, with not a little consternation. Respect for the ways of a church that is not yours is especially important in a funeral because you can disrupt the worship experience of the mourners and leave them with a very negative memory for the rest of their lives.

Finally, note that the phrase "do the funeral" is a common way of talking, along with other phrases such as "perform the funeral," "conduct the funeral," and "officiate at the funeral." How does one "do-perform-conduct-officiate at" a funeral? What exactly is a funeral anyway? In the most narrow sense, these shorthand phrases say that the minister is being asked to prepare and lead the funeral, seen as a worship service, which may happen in the church but happens far more often in a funeral home. In a broader sense, these phrases indicate that the minister is being asked to become involved with the bereaved in several ways, including pastoral visitation (though not always); any needed interaction with the family regarding funeral preparation; the funeral preparation itself; attending the visitation; leading the funeral service and committal, which is a brief ceremony following the funeral, usually at the gravesite, when the casket is to be placed in the grave; and attending a meal following the committal, if one is planned.

In a memorial service, the body is not present as it is in a funeral. When the body is cremated, the ashes of the body may be present in an urn if the cremation occurs before the service. Also, in a memorial service words of committal may happen in the service, whereas in a funeral the committal is at the cemetery following the service. An exception is when the urn containing the ashes is in the memorial service, and the committal is at the cemetery because the ashes are to be buried there.

Please be aware that there are differing funeral customs and procedures in different localities, and in different congregations, denominations, and religions, so that you will have to discover the differences in your location and church. For instance, if I talk about the visitation, it is something that most ministers will be experiencing before the funeral service, but it may happen differently in different localities. If I leave something out that is part of your funeral experience, or include something that is not part of your funeral experience, do not let it bother you. Instead, realize that if you move to a new part of the country, or sometimes even to a different part of your state, you will have to learn new customs. A funeral custom you may have assumed was universal can turn out to be something practiced only where you used to live and nowhere else. Because funeral homes are used for funerals today, and because there are a significant number of large funeral home chains around the country, it may seem that there is a growing homogenization in funeral practices. However, when sociologists study funerals within the larger context of contemporary life in the United States, changes having to do with funeral practices come into focus. For instance, following a study of the character of funeral practices in the United States, one sociologist concluded: "Change is at work not only in the mode of disposal of the dead but also in every sphere of funeralization as well–from the type of funeral establishment constructed to the emotional climate in which the funeral is conducted to the meaning imputed to death itself" (Fulton, 1994, 296).

Pastoral Visitation

I recently came upon an illustration in a popular magazine that communicates the change that ministers, church members, and acquaintances tend to undergo in their behavior toward distraught family members and very close friends of one who dies, upon learning of the death. The person who wrote this story is an engineer who reviews stereo equipment. He began one of his reviews this way:

> As part of my employer's never-ending attempts to transform me from an engineer into a manager, I am constantly being sent to seminars and courses, some of which are eminently practical...Others are more esoteric, like a recent seminar on "paradigm shifts." A paradigm shift, we were told, is a fundamental change in the way we look at things, arising from a change in a belief so inherent that it's unconscious. (Damkroger, 2001, 102)

Then this reviewer told a story illustrating such a paradigm shift:

> For example, imagine a long plane flight, late at night. A mother and two small children occupy the seats near you, and throughout the flight, the children are screaming–but the mother seems oblivious. After about two hours, you're getting pretty annoyed, so you complain to the flight attendants, who, inexplicably, also seem oblivious. They reply that the family is returning from the funeral of the children's beloved grandmother, the woman's mother. Instantly, annoyance becomes sympathy and empathy, and all you want to do–once you crawl out of the hole you wish you could sink into–is to help

in any way you can. Bingo! A paradigm shift. (Damkroger, 2001, 102)

Is such a "paradigm shift" not a good way to describe the change that often happens to people when they learn of a death? Even if you did not know the deceased personally, and even if you do not know the bereaved family members or friends personally, your tolerance for annoying behavior nevertheless increases dramatically, you become sympathetic and empathetic, and you want to offer help.

For the minister, this time when you find out about the death is a time for reaching out to those who have suffered a loss. This may happen on the day or night of the death, or it may happen after the family has been to the funeral home to make arrangements for the funeral on the day after the death and are gathering at someone's home afterward. There are many possible scenarios. In rare instances, a family member may not want the pastor to visit but will only see the pastor at the visitation before the funeral. At the same time, that person may have phone conversations with the pastor regarding funeral plans. Many times, most of the family may live out of town, or at least long distances away. They will be arriving on different days, at different times, so that there literally is no time when the family gathers with the pastor, either in the pastor's office or in someone's home. Instead, pastoral encounters with family and friends may happen piecemeal or sometimes not at all until the visitation and funeral.

What, then, should you do when you encounter the loved ones of the deceased? It may seem as if there's hardly any reason to address this, because well-known pastoral care and counseling wisdom on pastoral visitation is in effect. Listen well, exercise a ministry of presence, empathize, and avoid those awful platitudes so often resented, such as "It will be okay" and "It's for the best" and "It's God's will" (also see Mansell, 1998, 13–16 and his appendix A for a helpful care outline).

In the movie *Mass Appeal,* Jack Lemmon plays a middle-aged Roman Catholic priest who supervises a seminarian. They receive a phone call informing them that the mother of a middle-aged woman in the parish has died, so they make a pastoral visit together to see the grieving woman and her teenage daughter. The older priest sits in the living room with the woman, while the seminarian sits at the kitchen table with her daughter. The older priest shows us how not to care, by spending that precious time trying to talk the woman out of her grief.

After telling the priest that her mother died suddenly as she was entering the hospital, the woman, weeping, says, "I should have seen an attack coming."

The priest replies, "She was 78." He was implying that the woman should be glad that her mother lived such a long life, rather than beating herself up for not anticipating her mother's sudden attack.

"Her mother lived to be 89," the woman retorts.

The priest switches strategies, saying, "It was a fast and merciful death. Be thankful for that." His second strategy is as ineffective as the first. She will not be consoled.

It was not that he really expected her mood to shift from sorrow to thankfulness. Rather, his strategy reflected his overall approach to ministry, in which avoiding pain and conflict and trying to keep people happy by telling them what he thought they wanted to hear regardless of what he really thought, had become a way of life.

Meanwhile, the seminarian is sitting in anxious silence with the teenager. What should he say, if anything? After a few quiet moments, she bursts into tears. This scene seems reminiscent of a scene in the first part of Job, after he has lost his children, his servants, and his livestock: "Now when Job's three friends heard of all these troubles that had come upon him, each of them set out from his home…They met together to go and console and comfort him. When they saw him from a distance, they did not recognize him, and they raised their voices and wept aloud; they tore their robes and threw dust in the air upon their heads. They sat with him on the ground seven days and seven nights, and no one spoke a word to him, for they saw that his suffering was very great." (Job 2:11–13). Trying to talk a newly bereaved person out of grief is hardly comforting. Rather, this is a time for comforting presence.

Not every visit following a death will be the same. One cold winter night at 9:00 p.m., I received a phone call that a church member died. Though this person had been terminally ill, and his death had been imminent, there still was a strong sense of tragedy about it. A husband and father left behind his wife, children, siblings, parents, other relatives, and close friends, who also were church members. I felt that I should go to the house to see the family right then and there. I did not quite know what I would find when I got there, nor was I sure exactly what I would say. It was nearly 10:00 p.m. when I arrived after a long drive. What I did find was a house full of family and friends strewn through almost every room. There would be no sitting at the kitchen table on that night. Instead, the wife greeted me, and I expressed my condolences. Then I made my way through the house expressing my condolences to each of the children, the siblings, and the parents. Along the way, I was introduced to family members and friends I had not met before. After this, I had a choice to make. What should I do next?

One option was to find a seat somewhere and stay for a while, time that would be spent mostly just chatting with strangers who happened to be sitting nearby. I chose another option. I offered to have a prayer. Someone announced to the group that the minister was going to pray, so everyone became quiet, and those who had been in other rooms crowded around. I do not remember the exact content of my prayer, but

I do recall that I began by giving thanks for the life of the one who died, and I prayed for the family and for comfort and strength during the difficult days ahead. Following the prayer, I noticed that several people had begun crying quietly and were wiping their eyes. After a few minutes, I sensed that it was time for me to leave, so I said my good-byes and drove home. It was time for me to focus on the funeral.

Funeral Preparation

Funeral preparation primarily involves putting together the order of worship and the content of the funeral service and committal, or memorial service, just as the minister prepares the bulletin, prayers, and sermon for the regular Sunday worship service. Although a few authors provide possible funeral outlines for you to use, you should be familiar with the order of worship provided by your denomination. For instance, my denomination, the Presbyterian Church (USA), provides the *Book of Common Worship*, which contains a section titled "The Funeral: A Service of Witness to the Resurrection." This section contains prayers for comforting the bereaved, the order of worship for a funeral, resources for the committal, and numerous scripture readings for use in the funeral and committal. If you are a Master of Divinity student and you have not yet been involved with funerals, you should make it your business to discover the resources that your denomination provides for you to use in funeral preparation and leadership. Having this information can ease your anxiety and increase your confidence when you are faced with actual funerals.

Funeral preparation includes input from the family of the deceased when possible. Ideally, this means that you will have a second conversation with the family, or friends as the case may be, for the purpose of discussing the funeral (see Mansell, 1998, 16–20). This conversation can happen in the pastor's office or in a family member's home, but you also may have to gather needed information piecemeal depending on circumstances. Typically, you need to discuss special requests the family may have for the funeral, including music, scripture passages, and speakers. The family may not want music at the funeral, or they may want music but have no specific songs in mind, or they may want a favorite hymn of the deceased sung, or they may want a solo sung by a family member or friend. If the funeral is in the funeral home, there may be music before and at the end of the service, but if you want a hymn, you may have to copy it and bring it yourself. If the funeral is at your church, it will be much easier to have hymns as a matter of course. There also may be a favorite biblical passage you are asked to read, and a family member may be planning to speak at the funeral. Sometimes family members may have these things worked out before you speak to them, and other times it will be you who raises these questions with them so that they can call you later when they find out needed information. For example, if a relative coming from out of town is the one who may speak, they need to wait until this person arrives before letting you know for sure whether the person will speak.

Another important aspect of conversation with the family and friends involves listening to stories they want to tell about the deceased and even inviting them to share such stories. As one pastor observes: "I have often noted that family members revisit memories that are long past and humorously relive the experience" (Mansell, 1998, 18). In terms of funeral preparation, one reason to hear these stories is for possible use in the sermon, but it simultaneously relates to the grief process and mourning. In addition to learning family stories you did not already know, you can draw on your own experience of the deceased person. Sometimes your ability to articulate your experience of the deceased person in the funeral sermon can be quite meaningful, especially if the family members are unable to articulate their own stories.

There are some additional issues that accompany your funeral preparation, which should be mentioned briefly. Normally, you will have had a phone conversation with the funeral home so that you know basic information such as the day, time, and place of the visitation and funeral. If the deceased was a church member, either you or someone else should make sure that church members are informed of the death by means of the particular communication method your congregation has devised for such matters, such as a phone tree. If the funeral is going to be in the sanctuary of your church, make sure that the sanctuary is prepared for the funeral. This is the practical part of pastoral ministry that no one mentions. Whether there is a staff person to do it or whether you do it yourself, the doors have to be unlocked, the lights turned on, the sound system turned on, the thermostat adjusted, and even the floor swept or vacuumed if necessary.

The Visitation

The visitation, also called the viewing or calling, typically is on the evening before the funeral and most often is held at the funeral home. However, it can be on the day of the funeral and can be in the church. The ancestor of the visitation is the wake. *Merriam-Webster's Collegiate Dictionary* defines a wake as a "watch held over the body of a dead person prior to burial and sometimes accompanied by festivity." In the visitation, the body, which has been prepared for viewing, lies in an open casket, while the family members act as hosts to those who attend. The minister should be sure to attend, expressing condolences to the family members, like others who are there.

Often the visitation is where the minister will meet a family member who has just arrived from out of town. It also may be where the minister meets a relative or friend who will speak or sing at the funeral. The visitation may be the only place where the pastor has a chance to talk to one or more family members about some facet of the funeral or finally hear a story about the deceased that may find its way into the funeral sermon. Some families will place a group of family pictures and even memorabilia on display at the viewing, which provides a great opportunity for the pastor to hear family members or friends tell stories about the deceased person. This assumes, of course, that the family members are willing to talk about the deceased, but this is not always the case.

Ministers have no obligation to stay at the visitation for an extended period, though visitations can take on the cast of a family reunion. Indeed, there can be a family reunion of sorts as relationships are renewed. It would be a mistake to assume that all such reunions are positive. This is a time when family system dysfunction and existing tensions between family members are played out in the public arena, not only at the viewing but sometimes even at the time of the funeral service itself. More than one pastor has had to do some on-the-spot family crisis counseling on such occasions.

The Day of the Funeral

Never, ever be late for a funeral. Because you have been to the visitation at the funeral home, you have no excuse for not finding your way and figuring out how long the drive will take. I have found that arriving a half hour before the funeral allows me plenty of time to park the car, or get it placed in the funeral procession that will go to the cemetery, and then get ready to begin the service.

Whether the funeral is at the church or funeral home, the funeral director will take over following the benediction at the end of the funeral. Again, customs vary greatly. One thing you can do to put your mind at ease is call the funeral director or talk to that person at the visitation in order to clarify the usual procedures. Typically, if the funeral is in the funeral home, the funeral director has the entire congregation pass by the casket, which has remained open during the service, for a final farewell to the deceased, with the family going last. If the funeral is in the church, the casket is closed during the funeral service and the congregation does not file past the casket at the end of the service. The minister leads the procession to the hearse, walking in front of the casket. After the drive to the cemetery, the minister leads the procession from the hearse to the grave, or in some instances to a small chapel at the cemetery, for the committal.

After the committal, the mourners, including the pastor, often gather for a meal, so food must be mentioned. If you imagine that church members—church women, to be exact—across the country are spending long hours preparing a meal at their church following a funeral, you are probably living in some bygone era or know nothing about funerals today. Of course, it may be done sometimes upon request or according to a local custom. But very often, if there is going to be a meal, it is at a restaurant, and occasionally in someone's home. There is something rejuvenating about having a meal at this time. An extremely difficult event has just taken place, and somehow the meal allows the mourners to pull themselves together and have an ending to that event that is renewing.

Conclusion

Funeral time may only last a few days, but as you can see, it is a challenging time for you as a minister. When you agree to do a funeral, your own subjective response to the death, along with your various interactions with the bereaved, and your preparation for the funeral form a framework of events that not only lead up to the funeral but also contribute to the quality of care provided through it. This is only the beginning of the challenge, however. Now comes grief.

CHAPTER TWO

The Language of Loss

Let's say you are sitting in your office ready to prepare a funeral service for tomorrow. For a moment you think about the deceased, then your thoughts shift to the loved ones who will be at the funeral. You assume that they are grieving, because that's what people do who have lost someone to death. Yet, you recall that when you visited the spouse of the deceased person, you were surprised at the calmness and composure you encountered. Wasn't this person supposed to be crying, distraught, disoriented, like the person whose spouse you buried two months ago? This sure was different, and it raises a question for you. What exactly is grief if individuals can have very different reactions to the death of a loved one?

In a chapter addressing grief, the first lesson to learn is that grief must be placed within the context of a whole vocabulary having to do with situations involving death. I formerly used a whole cluster of words more or less interchangeably when dealing with a pastoral situation involving death. These words are *bereavement, loss, grief,* and *mourning.* I just assumed that they were different ways of referring to grief. Perhaps you have done this, too. In reality, these words have different meanings and refer to different aspects of losing someone to death. Together, they form a limited but potent vocabulary addressing this circumstance.

Bereavement

There appears to be no word or phrase in the English language that refers strictly to losing someone to death and nothing else, but *bereavement* comes close. According to the *Oxford English Dictionary* (used for all dictionary definitions unless otherwise specified), the word *bereavement* means, "The fact or state of being bereaved or deprived of anything." This does not tell us much except that being bereaved is the same as being deprived of something. So let's go to the word *bereaved* to see if its definition can shed more light on bereavement. *Bereaved* means being "deprived or robbed; taken away by force." Any possession can be robbed or taken by force. But there also is a more specific definition of bereaved. It can mean the experience of being "deprived by death of a near relative, or of one connected by some endearing tie." So, in the definition with which we are concerned, *bereavement* refers to the fact or state of being deprived of a family member or other person with whom you have an "endearing tie" due to the person's death.

As it is used here, the word *deprived* carries the connotation of being robbed, which brings us to the word *bereave.* This is an archaic form of the word no longer used in contemporary discourse, though understanding *bereaved* and *bereavement* without it would be impossible. If you bereave someone, you are robbing, plundering, or despoiling that person, or you are leaving the person "destitute, orphaned, or widowed." A still more archaic verb form of the word is *reave.* In addition to robbing, plundering, and despoiling, the meaning of *reave* is very basic in the sense of referring to the act of taking something away forcibly, not only in the material realm but also in spiritual matters. To *reave* can mean "to take or carry away (a person) *from* another, *from* earth, *to* heaven, etc.; also...to carry off to heaven; to take *away* from earth or this life."

You can see how *bereaved* is derived from *bereave* and *reave.* If you are bereaved, you are not the one taking something from another; instead you are the one who has something taken away from you, and from this life, as if by force. Specifically, another person is taken away from you through death. In this case, you become one of the bereaved, and you are in the state of bereavement.

Is bereavement something with which you can identify? Imagine having your home plundered while you were away. Upon your return, would you not feel surprised, stunned, angry, or afraid? Would you not feel that an injustice had taken place? Would you not want to seek justice and have your possessions returned? Would you want revenge? Would you feel as safe as you did before? Would you not worry about the same thing happening again? Before this crime, you lived happily oblivious to the possibility that it could happen to you. Now you are painfully aware of its reality, and you feel vulnerable. Perhaps, depending on the violence done to you, you might experience something like this, or you might try to shrug it off. In neither case, however, is bereavement neutral, leaving you in the same condition as before you became bereaved. Rather, it has a powerful impact on your life, as words such as *robbed, plundered,* and *despoiled* convey. Can the same be said of loss?

Loss

The word *loss* is used in many more ways than bereavement today. For instance, you may lose a game of checkers, or you may lose a hat, or you may lose heart. What, then, makes this word *loss* appropriate for referring to situations involving death?

It may be surprising that dictionary definitions of loss tend to begin with a focus on the thing that is lost rather than on the one doing the losing. For instance, the first definition of loss in the *Oxford English Dictionary* is "perdition, ruin, destruction." In this definition, something becomes lost in the sense of being destroyed or coming to ruin, such as a ship lost at sea. The use of *perdition* in this definition even takes loss into the theological realm in the sense that *perdition* can refer to "the condition of final spiritual ruin or damnation, the future condition of the wicked and finally impenitent or unredeemed; the fate of those in hell, eternal death." Yet, today when we say that someone's life has been lost, we normally are not saying that the person is wicked or condemned to eternal damnation in hell. Instead, we simply mean that the person is dead, like the more sanitized term *passed away.*

There also are definitions of loss referring to the survivors rather than the one who has died. In this sense a person is being "deprived by death" of a friend or relative. This experience may include regret, which in this context means feeling sorrow due to the loss. *Sorrow* means "distress of mind caused by loss...grief, deep sadness or regret." On an even stronger note, the loss may mean "to suffer severely by losing (usually a person)." Thus, we tend to say that a family member or friend has suffered a loss.

Contemporary pastoral theologians and psychotherapists tend to prefer the language of loss over that of bereavement. *Bereavement* mainly refers to death today, but there are many kinds of loss, all of which may give rise to grief. For instance, in *All Our Losses, All Our Griefs: Resources for Pastoral Care,* Kenneth Mitchell and Herbert Anderson identify six kinds of loss: material, relationship, intrapsychic, functional, role, and systemic loss. They identify loss due to death as one type of relationship loss (37–38), but as their book title indicates, they are concerned with "all our losses," not just loss due to death. Psychotherapist Therese Rando divides loss into physical loss and psychosocial loss, also called symbolic loss (1993, 20–22). Physical loss is similar to Mitchell and Anderson's material loss, but psychosocial loss is such a broad category that it includes their other five kinds of loss.

Rando also discusses what is called secondary loss, which she defines as "a physical or psychosocial loss that coincides with or develops as a consequence of the initial loss" (20). When the initial loss is a death, a secondary physical loss can be as immediate and fundamental as the loss of "the loved one's presence" (20). Or it can be a loss happening after some time has elapsed following the death, such as having to "relocate due to economic hardship after the death" (20). Secondary psychosocial losses following the initial loss due to death can be myriad:

The mourner typically sustains much more than physical loss after a death. Loved ones play many roles in an individual's life. For instance, a spouse may be one's lover, best friend, helpmate, confidant, co-parent, social partner, housemate, traveling companion, business associate, career supporter, auto repair person, housekeeper, and "other half," among other roles. With the death, the mourner loses someone to fill these roles and to gratify the needs and sustain the feelings associated with them in the particular way the deceased did. In addition, the mourner loses a view of the world and the countless feelings, thoughts, behavior and interaction patterns, hopes, wishes, fantasies, dreams, assumptions, expectations, and beliefs that required the loved one's presence. The deprivation of the gratification the loved one once provided, the unfulfilled needs, the unreinforced behavior patterns, the unmet expectations, the emotional wishes, and the role relationships left empty are all examples of secondary psychosocial losses associated with the death. (20–21)

Such innumerable possible losses can have a powerful impact on the life of a bereaved person because, as Rando points out, each of these secondary losses "initiates its own grief and mourning reactions" (20). It is not just the quantity of secondary losses but their ability to generate additional grief and mourning that makes them so powerful.

C. S. Lewis tells what experiencing secondary losses is like, only with fewer words, writing as if to his deceased wife: "Did you ever know, dear, how much you took away with you when you left? You have stripped me even of my past, even of the things we never shared. I was wrong to say the stump was recovering from the pain of the amputation. I was deceived because it has so many ways to hurt me that I discover them only one by one" (1961, 48).

Grief

Like loss, and to some extent bereavement, grief has several definitions that do not refer to situations of death. There is one definition, however, in the *Oxford English Dictionary*, that does take loss into account. It starts out in a general way, defining grief as "mental pain, distress, or sorrow." However, before loss can be taken into account and become part of the larger definition, this qualification is needed: "In mod. [modern] use in a more limited sense." Then, after the qualification comes the larger definition: "Deep or violent sorrow, caused by loss or trouble; a keen or bitter feeling of regret for something lost; remorse for something done, or sorrow for mishap to oneself or others." In *Merriam-Webster's Collegiate Dictionary* (1998), one definition of grief actually refers to bereavement, though tentatively. Grief is defined as "deep and poignant distress caused by or as if by bereavement."

Dictionaries show us that our use of the word *grief* primarily in situations of death is a Johnny-come-lately in the English language. The main responsibility for narrowing the use of *grief* to situations of death and other serious losses lies with psychiatry, and through psychiatry with the mental health industry as a whole. Through their writings, psychiatrists and psychologists have claimed the experience of bereaved people so strongly that it never occurs to us to conceive of bereavement in any way but psychologically or to use any other expressions than grief to characterize the reaction to bereavement, even though bereavement is not a category of mental illness.

Contemporary psychology controls our understanding of grief as much as Microsoft controls computer software. Experiencing "deep or violent sorrow" because a loved person has died does not inspire theological reflection on the nature of finitude and relationships as much as it leads to the application of some psychiatric model of grief. Poetry, philosophical thought, and biblical stories provide mere illustrations of grief understood psychologically, and they dare not contradict it. Where does this leave ministers, who must conduct funerals using the language and concepts of the Christian faith?

On the one hand, it leaves us needing to learn everything we can about grief as it is understood psychologically, because this is how bereavement is talked about today, and psychiatrists do have very helpful information about grief. Pastors have no excuse for being ignorant of grief understood psychologically. On the other hand, the utter dominance of the psychological understanding of grief leaves us needing to resist captivity by it. I say this from the standpoint of having the responsibility of conducting funerals, not as a psychiatrist but as a Christian pastor. There is nothing quite like standing in front of a group of bereaved people, ready to begin a funeral service, experiencing an almost eerie quietness in the room, knowing that what happens in the funeral that day will leave an indelible mark on the memory of the worshipers. Is grief present? It saturates the air. But the readings, the prayers, and the songs cannot be reduced to a psychological lesson in how to grieve; nor can the mourners be viewed as receiving some kind of group therapy in ceremonial garb. So the discussion of grief next, as well as the discussion of mourning, is presented in the twofold spirit of the importance of learning about grief understood psychologically and the freedom of resistance to captivity that would close off the possibility of incorporating the psychological understanding of grief appropriately in the service of the Christian ministry of funerals.

For the past half century, pastoral theologians have been in the forefront of introducing ministers to the psychological understanding of grief. One of the first to do this was Paul E. Irion in a book that has become a classic in the literature of pastoral care and counseling, *The Funeral and the Mourners: Pastoral Care of the Bereaved,* published in 1954.

You might assume that this is merely a historical citation, and instead you want to learn the contemporary understanding of grief. Well, I have some news for you. In the realm of writings about grief, it seems as if time has almost, but not quite, stood still. There are important psychiatric works on grief that have been written since 1954, and they get added to the list of authorities in contemporary writings. Yet, no matter how much time passes, the same exceedingly similar discussions of grief, and introductions of the same authoritative authors on grief, happen again and again. For instance, Irion begins his psychological discussion of bereavement by introducing Sigmund Freud and his famous paper "Mourning and Melancholia." Next he mentions Melanie Klein, another psychiatrist. The third psychiatrist he discusses, Erich Lindemann, has, like Freud, become a household name in grief literature because of his study of bereaved patients following a disastrous fire in 1942, when a crowded Boston nightclub called the Coconut Grove burst into flames. Freud, Klein, and Lindemann continue to be important contributors to the understanding of grief, but many more authors whose work on grief is discussed routinely have joined them, such as John Bowlby, whose three-volume work *Attachment and Loss* (1969, 1973, 1980) is a landmark in grief literature.

Grief as a Complex of Feelings

Irion defines grief as "primarily an emotion, or more accurately, a complex of feelings. Modern psychological studies have shown that feelings of guilt, hostility, fear, bewilderment, and loneliness often accompany the feeling of sorrow which we recognize as a characteristic of bereavement" (29). The thing evoking this "complex of feelings" is of course the loss of someone due to death. For this reason, Irion also says that grief involves "a severe disruption of the structure of the personality because of the loss which has been suffered" (39). Like Irion, Mitchell and Anderson focus on emotion in their definition of grief: "Grief is the normal but bewildering cluster of ordinary human emotions arising in response to a significant loss, intensified and complicated by the relationship to the person or the object lost" (1983, 54). Rando, however, defines the grief reaction more broadly as "the process of experiencing the psychological, behavioral, social, and physical reactions to the perception of loss" (1993, 22).

Irion discusses several features of grief that are written about today as they were in 1954. The first of these is tearfulness: "One of the most common elements of the grief reaction is tearfulness. Grief...is a painful experience which is often accompanied by periods of weeping. Thinking of or talking about the deceased appears to be the stimulus of the tearfulness" (42). He carefully points out that not all people are the same. Some people hardly seem to cry at all, maintaining great control over their emotions, whereas others unleash a flood of tears.

Second are bewilderment and loneliness. Irion describes bewilderment as the experience of losing the meaningfulness of life because the deceased was so much a part of it. "Thus, the whole pattern of life is upset. This confusion of the stuff of daily existence puts the mourner somewhat out of touch with reality" (44). He then goes on to describe the bewildered person as "in a daze, apparently lost, even amid familiar surroundings" (44). Loneliness is closely related to bewilderment when the loss is so disruptive to the life of the bereaved person. It includes a painful sense of emptiness. Or, more pointedly, Irion quotes another pastoral theologian, William Rogers: "Our loved one is gone and there is only an aching void where once he was. The emptiness and change that have come to our lives are a bitter portion indeed" (45, and see Rogers, 1950).

Third is fear. Irion points first to the fear of death itself, which is an "ontological fear"(46) having roots in human finitude. This fear becomes personalized in the twofold sense of pertaining to the deceased and also to the one who is grieving. He also mentions fear of the dead, which may be largely unconscious and provide motivation to "placate the spirit of the deceased" through "effusive demonstrations of affection and honor, or lavish funerals" (46). A third kind of fear is the "dread of the experiences which accompany death: the loneliness, the loss, the insecurity, the pain of mourning" (47). This is the fear of secondary losses approaching on the horizon following the death.

Fourth is ambivalence. This means that the bereaved person can have "simultaneous contradictory emotions" (48) about the deceased, in which one of the emotions is positive and one is negative. One minute you feel one way, but the next minute you feel the other way. It puts you in a position of indecision. For instance, recall my example in the first chapter about the church member who feared that there would be no one to bury him if I went on vacation. What I described as my mixed feelings of sorrow over his death on the one hand and my irritation on the other is an instance of ambivalence, in the sense of having contradictory emotions simultaneously.

Fifth is hostility. This is the negative side of ambivalence that emerges in grief. "Hostile feelings may either blend in with feelings of affection and love or alternate with them. Just as in life interpersonal relationships are subject to varying degrees of harmony and conflict, feelings toward the deceased party of the relationship may take on different colorations" (49).

Sixth is guilt. A bereaved person may feel guilty for having hostility toward the deceased. This can take the form of self-blame for such things as "not giving the deceased proper care during a period of illness, for not perfectly fulfilling marital obligations, or for contributing in some way to the cause of death" (51). As you can imagine from your own life experience, there are a wide range of possibilities regarding the circumstances that may generate guilt, and guilt may or may not have a basis in fact. In addition to guilt, Mitchell and Anderson add shame to the discussion (1983, 73–78), which undoubtedly needs further exploration in the realm of grief.

Seventh is idealization. Oftentimes, when the bereaved are remembering their loved one, any negative qualities of the deceased person are set aside, whereas positive qualities are brought out and enhanced. "This remembering activity is often highly colored by accentuating the virtues and positive values of the deceased" (Irion, 1954, 55).

Grief as a Process

Although grief may be identified as a complex or cluster of feelings, it does not behave like the feelings that come and go in everyday life. So there need to be additional ways of describing and understanding grief. The main way probably is familiar to you. It is called the grief process. Numerous authors have described this process, but I would like to mention just one as an example, pastoral theologian Wayne Oates. In 1955, one year after Irion's book *The Funeral and the Mourners* came out, a book by Oates was published, *Anxiety in Christian Experience*, which includes a chapter on grief. As a process, grief is seen in terms of a series of stages through which the bereaved person passes. The stages describe ways the bereaved person attempts to cope with loss, beginning at the point when the person learns about the death and ending when the person accepts the loss fully enough to become reintegrated into life without the deceased. Oates describes the process this way:

- The shocking blow of the loss in itself. You are assaulted with the objective reality of the death, but you cannot absorb this reality subjectively all at once. You may faint, or you may act mechanically for a while until you can begin absorbing the news.
- The numbing effect of the shock. Oates compares numbing to the "freezing" power of a local anesthetic. "This seems to be nature taking care of the individual by anesthetizing them emotionally. The feelingful reality of the blow will become broken to them gradually."
- The struggle between fantasy and reality. In order to describe this struggle, Oates compares it to an amputation. Just as the amputee goes on acting as if the lost body part were still there for a time, so the "grief-stricken person struggles over accepting the reality of the loss" and may act as if the lost person were still there.
- The breakthrough of a flood of grief. The wall of fantasy, as Oates describes it, becomes broken, which allows the feeling of grief to come rushing over you. "From a psychological point of view, this is a catharsis of the wound of grief."

- Selective memory and stabbing pain. Even a flood levels off eventually. The pain of grief becomes less intense and becomes tied more closely to memories of the deceased occurring during the course of daily life. "He may be walking down the street and see someone who reminds him of the person for whom he is grieving. The pleasantness of the remembrance of the loved one is rudely interrupted with the reality: 'She is gone!' 'She is dead!'"
- The acceptance of loss and the reaffirmation of life itself. Oates describes this final stage as a kind of reversal accomplished as the person discovers new meaning in life. The person is "first rejecting life in the face of death and then accepting death in the face of life." You accomplish this acceptance and reaffirmation of life "by having taken the lost image of the loved one" into your concept of yourself, or you have internalized it. (1955, 51–56)

Therese Rando uses the language of phases rather than stages when describing the grief process. In Rando's model, the first phase is avoidance. This phase corresponds surprisingly well to the first three stages Oates describes. The second phase is confrontation, which corresponds to some extent with Oates's stages four and five, though it is far more comprehensive and is based on more contemporary resources than were available to Oates in the 1950s. The third phase is accommodation, somewhat similar to Oates's stage six, though of course not identical. She goes on to acknowledge that grieving people may move back and forth between the phases, depending on a variety of factors, and that not every person experiences each and every reaction found in the three phases (1993, 30).

One part of the grief process difficult to write about is its fluctuations. It is commonplace for people to question the veracity of grief seen as a process because they do not see others or themselves going through stages of grief in a lockstep fashion, or according to any particular timetable. Contrary to what has been popular belief, even in pastoral care and counseling, the notion that the grief process is completed within one year is patently false in many, many cases. If grief were this predictable, its progress would have to be very linear and the ups and downs in intensity would have to be very short term, declining consistently until they were gone within twelve months.

However, the grief process does not proceed in a linear fashion toward an end at a predetermined time, such as a year. According to Rando, "despite the widespread societal, and unfortunately often clinical, myth that grief and mourning decline in a linear fashion over time, this simply is not the case" (1993, 62). She goes on to cite research showing quite a different picture than linear decline. Having done research with bereaved parents whose children had died of cancer, she found that

"78 percent of the bereavement symptoms measured diminished from Year 1 to Year 2 after the death. However, they rose again during Year 2 to Year 3!" (62). She also cites similar results by other grief researchers, showing significant fluctuations in the grief process among grieving parents over several years. Differences in patterns of fluctuation between males and females also came to light in this research, having implications for the relationship between the parents literally for years following the death of their child (62).

It also is highly questionable whether there can be any truly final stage in which grief ends and is no more, for grief and mourning can become part of a person's life at some level even though the person does move on and lives fruitfully in the years following the death of a loved one. In addition, there are many variables affecting the way grief is experienced, including such things as anticipatory grief, when the initial shock comes from learning that someone you care about is terminally ill; different personality types of the bereaved; the family history of the bereaved; the relationship to the deceased; the kind of death; and the circumstances surrounding it.

In reality, those who write about the grief process often are quite sensitive to these kinds of grief issues and may be very clear that the grief process should not be viewed as something everyone goes through in lockstep or within the same amount of time. For instance, Therese Rando, before describing her version of the grief process, says, "Without question, commonalities exist within the human experience; equally without question, idiosyncratic variations occur. The astute caregiver identifies and responds to both, recognizing that even universals are experienced distinctly and individually" (1993, 30).

You may not want to pigeonhole someone as being in a particular stage of grief, but at the same time the grief process, as written about by some author, may helpfully describe a grief experience the person is having. In addition, it not only puts that experience in a larger context of other grief experiences associated with the grief process, but also provides a goal to work toward. Mitchell and Anderson put it this way:

> Grieving is a process moving toward a receding goal, a goal never fully reached; the relative "normality" of the process is judged by its effectiveness in helping the grieving person to approach that goal as closely as possible. The goals of grieving include these: to enable a person to live a life relatively unencumbered by attachments to the person or thing lost; to remake emotional attachments; to recognize and live with the reality of the loss and the feelings occasioned by it. Moving

toward these goals can involve a variety of activities, and any activity that moves one in this direction is "normal." (1983, 86)

Grief as Separation Anxiety

Oates did not follow Irion in calling grief a complex of feelings. Instead, he identified grief as one kind of anxiety. Pastoral theologian David Switzer went much further than Oates in developing this view of grief in his book *The Dynamics of Grief,* published in 1970. Switzer defines anxiety as "fear of separation" (94). Accordingly, when a person loses someone to death with whom they have been "closely related emotionally" (93), then the core of that person's grief, or the "major dynamic of the inner experience of grief" (93), is anxiety, or the fear resulting from separation.

When this route of understanding grief is taken, a question naturally arises concerning what it is that the grieving person fears following the separation due to death. The answer is found in Switzer's interpersonal model of personality. Drawing on the work of psychologists and that of psychiatrists such as John Bowlby, Switzer identifies the origin of anxiety in the infant-and-mother relationship, in which the infant depends on the mothering person not only for survival but also for development of the self. No matter how old people get, they still need to maintain relationships with emotionally significant others, and the loss of such relationships can be experienced as a threat to the self, even a threat to its existence. To make a long psychological story short, what a grieving person fears, having been separated from an emotionally significant person through death, is "the destruction of one's own self, or death" (1970, 102).

If the core of grief is separation anxiety, what about other aspects of grief, such as those listed by Irion and by Mitchell and Anderson? The view of grief as separation anxiety does not mean that other aspects of grief are ignored. Switzer also discusses guilt, ambivalence, and hostility, showing how they, too, are forms that anxiety assumes in grief (1970, 118–44). The question is whether anxiety can count as the source of all grief feelings, or whether there are multiple sources.

Grief Models as Pastoral Resources

Fortunately, ministers are not forced to choose among the different ways of understanding grief. Rather, they can draw on several ways of understanding it, such as the three that have been mentioned. In one instance, a pastor may be most helpfully informed by having at hand knowledge of several different emotions involved in grief, regardless of their origins in human development. In another instance, knowledge of the grief process may be most helpful, whereas in yet another instance, knowledge of grief seen in relation to personality development may be most helpful.

Mourning

Once again, the dictionary prevents us from assigning only one meaning to a word. According to the *Oxford English Dictionary*, *mourn* and its related form, *mourning,* can have several meanings. For instance, to mourn can mean "to have a painful longing" for the person who has died. It is easy to resonate with this understanding of the word *mourn*, which describes the emotion associated with losing someone to death. It is straightforward and pervasive, like the word *sorrow.*

Similarly, *mourning* can be simply another word for grief and sorrow. This definition says that mourning is "the feeling or the expression of sorrow for the death of a person." Note, however, that there is a difference between feeling sorrow, or the emotion of grief, and expressing it. Feeling sorrow is an inner, subjective experience of emotion, which may or may not be expressed. Expressing sorrow involves the outward manifestation of the emotion through some behavior, such as crying.

During the last half century, mourning quite often has referred to this outward expression of grief being experienced subjectively, rather than being a synonym of grief. In this case, the subjective experience is named grief, whereas outwardly expressing this experience is named mourning. Many authors distinguish between grief and mourning this way (for instance, see Parks, 1972, 108n; and Fitzgerald, 1994, 30). However, if *mourning* deserves to be part of the vocabulary of loss important to pastors, there must be more to consider.

Human beings typically have more than one way of expressing emotions, ways that may be very different, and this is true of mourning. To mourn also can mean "to exhibit the conventional signs of grief for a period following the death of a person; *esp.* to wear mourning garments," which traditionally have been dark clothes worn for a specific period. But what does it mean to say that something is a "sign" of grief? One definition of *mourning* indicates that a "sign" is the same as a "conventional or ceremonial manifestation of sorrow for the death of a person." You would think that this understanding of *sign* points us directly to funerals, but definitions of *mourn* and *mourning* do not include any explicit references to funerals, with two exceptions.

One is found in the definition of the related word *mourner.* A mourner can be not only one who "mourns the death of a friend or relation" but also one who "attends a funeral out of respect or affection for the deceased." Hence Irion's appropriate title, *The Funeral and the Mourners.* The second exception brings us to another definition of the word *mourn*. To mourn can mean "to lament the death of someone." In this sense, *lament* is just another word for mourning seen as an expression of grief, except for adding the quality of being a passionate, profound, demonstrative expression of grief as opposed to a mild expression. However, lament also can be another word for mourning in the sense of being a conventional or ceremonial expression of mourning that is explicitly associated with funerals. In this ceremonial sense, lament is "a song of grief," also called an elegy, which is a "funeral song or lament for the dead."

There is a huge difference between feeling your chest become heavy while tears well up in your eyes, singing a lament, or choosing to wear black for a time. It is the difference between a surge of emotion finding immediate expression and intentional acts that take planning. Both these things involve expressing grief, but neither can be reduced to the other.

The Psychological Understanding of Mourning

In many instances, the ceremonial understanding of mourning, seen as a social view, has been set aside in psychology in favor of a focus on mourning seen as the immediate, emotional expression of grief. Yet, in contemporary psychology, mourning can be seen as more than just a word for expressing grief.

Rando distinguishes between mourning seen as the mere expression of grief and mourning seen as a more active response needed for healthy grieving:

> Mere expression of reaction to the loss is too passive. There must be active movement and change if a major loss is to be processed, worked through, reconciled, and integrated into a mourner's life, and if that individual is to be able to continue on in a healthy fashion in the new life without the loved one. Thus, grief is a necessary but not sufficient condition to come to successful accommodation of loss. The active processes of mourning are required as well. (1993, 23)

She defines mourning in this more active sense as "conscious and unconscious processes and courses of action" (1993, 23) that help the grieving person deal effectively with the deceased, with the person's own self and with the external world. Rando says that view has its roots in the psychoanalytic tradition "of focusing on intrapsychic work" (23), while expanding on it by including "adaptive behaviors necessitated by the loss of the loved one" (23; and see 79–85 for a clarifying discussion of Freud's view of mourning).

According to Rando, mourning promotes three operations. The first operation focuses on the deceased: "The first operation promoted by mourning is the undoing of the psychosocial ties binding the mourner to the loved one" (23). The second operation focuses on the mourner: "In the second operation, mourning processes help the survivor adapt to the loss" (23). The third operation focuses on the external world: "The third and final operation promoted by mourning helps the mourner learn how to live in a healthy way in the new world without the deceased" (23).

The specific mourning processes enable a bereaved person to accomplish these three operations Rando calls the six "R" processes, which she presents in a brief outline before discussing them in detail:

> **Recognize** the loss
> > Acknowledge the loss
> > Understand the death (reasons for the death)
>
> **React** to the separation
> > Experience the pain
> > Feel, identify, accept, and give some form of expression to all
> > > the psychological reactions to the loss
> >
> > Identify and mourn secondary losses
>
> **Recollect** and re-experience the deceased and the relationship
> > Review and remember realistically
> > Revive and re-experience the feelings
>
> **Relinquish** the old attachments to the deceased and the old
> assumptive world
>
> **Readjust** to move adaptively into the new world without forgetting
> the old
> > Revise the assumptive world
> > Develop a new relationship with the deceased
> > Adopt new ways of being in the world
> > Form a new identity
>
> **Reinvest** (1993, 45, and see 46–60)

Rando says that the R processes are rooted in psychiatrist Erich Lindemann's concept of grief work (1993, 90). According to Lindemann, "The duration of a grief reaction seems to depend on the success with which a person does the grief work—namely, emancipation from the bondage to the deceased, readjustment to the environment in which the deceased is missing, and the formation of new relationships" (1979, 64).

Psychiatrists and psychologists, along with those in pastoral care and counseling, have written about grief work for many years. However, the use of this terminology has left us with an unhelpful ambiguity in our use of the word *grief.* Sometimes it means the subjective emotions bereaved people experience. Sometimes it means the grief process, and sometimes it means grief work. Grief authors often move among these three uses of *grief* in their discussions, which is confusing. For this reason, the word *mourning* is helpful. When *mourning* as Rando describes it can be used instead of the phrase *grief work*, it takes pressure off the word *grief* and provides for greater clarity in grief discussions.

When mourning is seen in terms of active processes needed for grieving, there can be no doubt that *mourning* should be included in the vocabulary of loss available for pastors to use. In this view, every bereaved person is seen as needing to mourn, to put the mourning processes into practice for the purpose of moving through the grief process effectively.

Complicated Mourning

As you probably have gathered by now, bereavement is a complex and potentially vast subject. This makes it all the more difficult to say when a bereaved person is grieving and mourning normally versus pathologically. Many writers shy away from such distinctions, yet still find themselves addressing instances when a grieving person needs professional help, for instance when there is increased vulnerability to such difficulties as mental and physical illness, substance abuse, and even death. So from the standpoint of ministers who deal with bereaved people in their pastoral ministry, it does not make much sense to omit this reality from the discussion of mourning.

Although it is not perfect, the language of uncomplicated and complicated mourning avoids the pitfall of labeling bereaved people as normal or abnormal, sick or well, while still providing a way to understand exceptionally difficult bereavement situations. Rando uses the six R processes discussed earlier as the measuring stick by which to judge whether mourning is uncomplicated or complicated. Simply put, in uncomplicated mourning, the bereaved individual is able to put all six active mourning processes into practice in a way that enables the person to move through the grief process. Though grief and mourning can take place over several years and are quite variable, in complicated mourning the bereaved individual is not able to put all six mourning processes into practice fruitfully no matter how many years are involved. Instead, "there is some compromise, distortion, or failure of one or more of the six 'R' processes of mourning" (1993, 149). The result is that the bereaved individual is not able to move through the grief process and suffers the consequences.

All complicated mourning is not the same. Rando identifies four different outcomes of loss associated with complicated mourning:

1. Symptoms of complicated mourning. This includes any aspect of grief, whether psychological, behavioral, social, or physical, which becomes more intense, prolonged, or distorted than is usually experienced in uncomplicated mourning. Or conversely, the absence of some aspect of grief can be a tip-off that mourning is becoming complicated.

2. A syndrome of complicated mourning. This is when a whole group of symptoms, or aspects of grief, are occurring together and become a recognizable condition. Rando discusses seven syndromes, including absent mourning, delayed mourning, inhibited mourning, distorted mourning, conflicted mourning, unanticipated mourning, and chronic mourning.

3. A mental or physical disorder that is diagnosable. The most common mental disorder associated with grief is a mood disorder or one of various types of depression. It is tricky to distinguish between grief and depression many times, but they should not be collapsed into the same thing. Rando contends that there has been too much focus on depression and that anxiety disorders are more prevalent in relation to complicated mourning than is generally recognized.

4. Death. The increased risk of mortality is the most extreme outcome of loss associated with complicated mourning. Suicide is the most well-known example, but there are many indirect means of self-destruction.

Note that the language of uncomplicated and complicated mourning gives way to the more explicit clinical language of symptoms and syndromes, which is appropriate given that Rando is writing for psychotherapists, to help them deal with bereaved clients and patients. Although pastors will not be practicing psychotherapy, they still need to be aware of the reality that bereavement can result in extremely serious and difficult outcomes, even years after the death has occurred.

Conclusion

Bereavement, loss, grief, and *mourning* form a vocabulary for ministers who must conduct funerals for church members and others who have lost a family member or friend to death. *Bereavement* not only communicates how difficult losing someone to death can be, through its robbing and plundering imagery, it provides a name for the condition of having lost someone to death. *Loss* is used similarly to *bereavement* but is a more flexible word, especially because it provides a way to talk about secondary losses. *Grief* is the name for the reactions of a person who has become bereaved. However, it is bursting at the seams because it is required to contain the many diverse features associated with these reactions. It may be too much to ask one word to cover so many bases in situations lasting literally for years. This is one reason that *mourning* is included in the vocabulary of loss. It provides a way for pastors to understand and talk about several things, including the emotional expression of grief, the active psychological and adaptive processes facilitating grief, and the conventional and ceremonial ways of expressing grief. In addition, it provides a way to talk about serious difficulties occurring when the mourning processes are not being put into practice fruitfully, and, finally, it provides a name for those who attend funerals.

CHAPTER THREE

The First Phase of Grief

A minister who cares for bereaved people before a funeral and then conducts the funeral is encountering people during the very earliest part of grief. Yet discussions of grief invariably include the psychological understanding of grief as a whole, which is a massive undertaking covering several years of a grieving person's life. Consequently, in most grief discussions there is space to give the initial part of grief only the most cursory attention.

Ministers should know more about the initial part of grief than can be conveyed through a discussion of the entire grief process. So in this chapter the very first part of grief, from the point of learning about the death through the funeral, will be the focus. The work of psychotherapist Therese Rando will be drawn upon primarily, but not exclusively, for addressing the definition of grief, the first phase of grief, and causes of variations in grief reactions. Although these issues are not new in themselves, confining the discussion to grief from the point of learning about a death through the funeral allows for a focus that should be helpful to ministers who conduct funerals.

Defining Grief

Defining grief is just an entry point into a maze of psychological perspectives on what human beings go through when someone they care about dies. Although the psychological understanding of grief typically starts out with a definition focusing on emotions, it quickly moves on to personality difficulties, stages of grief, physical reactions such as tears and potential medical difficulties, attempts to account for diversity in grief, and complicated grief. How can any definition do justice to the journey of grief human beings take, often in very unique ways?

Although no definition can be expected to include virtually all aspects of grief within its bounds, it is possible to define grief in a way that includes more of what bereaved people experience before and during funerals. Therese Rando offers such a definition, which was mentioned in chapter 2. According to her, grief is "the process of experiencing the psychological, behavioral, social, and physical reactions to the perception of loss" (1993, 22). A strength of this definition for pastors is that it encourages us not to discount behavioral, social, or physical aspects of what we are experiencing of bereaved people, as opposed to focusing too exclusively on emotions. At the same time, emotions in the definition are just as important as ever but are included under the psychological category. Let's look at each of the four areas.

The Psychological Response

The psychological response contains four different features, including affects (the psychological name for emotions), cognitions, perceptions, and defenses and/or attempts at coping. Rando provides an extensive list under each of the four features, describing their content. These lists are shown below. Under perceptions, for instance, she includes such things as "development of a perceptual set for the deceased" and "feeling as if something is about to happen." Also, there are some terms in multiple lists.

In her discussion, Rando also includes a religious/philosophical/ spiritual feature under the psychological category, saying that it, too, is seriously affected in the acutely grieved mourner (see 22, 40). She implies that it is a fifth feature under the psychological category. However, as we can see below, she actually places this feature under cognitions in the psychological category, as "spiritual confusion, alienation, rejection" or, conversely, "increased spirituality."

PSYCHOLOGICAL RESPONSES

(quoted from Rando, 1993, Table 2.2, 36–39)

Affects

- Separation pain, sadness, sorrow, anguish
- Anxiety, panic, fear, vulnerability, insecurity
- Yearning, pining, longing
- Helplessness; powerlessness; feelings of being out of control, victimized, overwhelmed
- Anger, hostility, irritability, intolerance, impatience
- Guilt, self-reproach, regret
- Depression, hopelessness, despair
- Anhedonia, apathy, restricted range of affect
- Frustration
- Fear of going crazy

- Emotional lability, hypersensitivity
- Deprivation, mutilation, violation
- Loneliness
- Abandonment
- Ambivalence
- Relief

Cognitions

- Disbelief
- Bewilderment
- Disorganization, confusion, distractibility
- Preoccupation with the deceased, obsession, rumination
- Impaired concentration, comprehension, mental functioning, memory, decision making
- Cognitive dissonance, meaninglessness, senselessness, disillusionment, aimlessness
- Spiritual confusion, alienation, rejection; increased spirituality
- Lowered self-esteem, feelings of inadequacy
- Pessimism
- Diminished self-concern
- Decreased interest, motivation, initiative, direction

Perceptions

- Feelings of unreality, depersonalization, derealization, dissociation
- Development of a perceptual set for the deceased
- Paranormal experiences pertaining to the deceased (e.g., visual or auditory hallucinations, sense of presence)
- Feeling as if something is about to happen

Defenses and/or Attempts at Coping

- Shock, numbness, absence of emotions
- Avoidance or repression of thoughts, feelings, or memories associated with the deceased or painful reactions to the loss
- Denial
- Searching behavior (for the deceased)
- Protest
- Regression
- Search for meaning
- Identification with the deceased
- Dreams of the deceased
- Feelings of unreality, depersonalization, derealization, dissociation

The Behavioral Response

The behavioral response involves the "personal action, conduct, or demeanor" (22) of the bereaved. It does not contain a subset of features, but such things as "social withdrawal" and "crying and tearfulness" are listed.

BEHAVIORAL RESPONSES
(quoted from Rando, 1993, Table 2.2, 36–39)

- Searching behavior (for the deceased)
- Restless hyperactivity, searching for something to do, heightened arousal, agitation, exaggerated startle response, hypervigilance, hypomanic behavior
- Social withdrawal
- Disorganized activity, absentminded behavior
- Increased intake of medicine and/or psychoactive substances
- Loss of patterns of social interaction (e.g., dependency, clinginess, avoidance of being alone)
- Crying and tearfulness
- Anorexia or appetite disturbance leading to weight loss or gain
- Sleep disturbance (too little, too much, interrupted)
- Tendency to sigh
- Decreased interest, motivation, initiative, direction, and energy for relationships and organized patterns of activity
- Decreased effectiveness and productivity in functioning (personal, social, work)
- Avoidance of or adherence to people, situations, and stimuli reminiscent of the deceased
- Self-destructive behaviors (e.g., accident-prone behavior, high-risk behavior such as fast driving)
- Acting-out behaviors, impulsive behaviors
- Hyposexuality or hypersexuality
- Change in lifestyle
- Hiding grief for fear of driving others away
- Clinging behavior
- Grief spasms

The Social Response

The social response involves "reactions to and interactions with others" (22). It does not contain a subset of features either, but such things as "criticality toward others" and "loss of patterns of social interaction" are listed. Below are nine social responses.

SOCIAL RESPONSES

(quoted from Rando, 1993, Table 2.2, 36–39)

- Lack of interest in other people and in usual activities due to preoccupation with the deceased
- Social withdrawal
- Decreased interest, motivation, initiative, direction, and energy for relationships and organized patterns of activity
- Boredom
- Criticality toward others and other manifestations of anger or irritation with others
- Loss of patterns of social interaction
- Feeling alienated, detached, or estranged from others
- Jealousy of others without loss
- Dependency on others, clinginess, and avoidance of being alone

The Physical Response

The physical response involves "bodily symptoms and physical health" (22). It contains three features, including biological signs of depression, symptoms indicative of anxiety and hyperarousal, and other physiological symptoms. For instance, under biological signs of depression are such things as "fatigue, lethargy" and "sleep disturbance."

PHYSICAL RESPONSES

(quoted from Rando, 1993, Table 2.2, 36–39)

Symptoms Indicative of Biological Signs of Depression

- Anorexia or appetite disturbance leading to weight loss or gain
- Decreased interest, motivation, initiative, direction, and energy
- Depressed mood
- Anhedonia, apathy, restricted range of affect
- Impaired concentration, mental functioning, memory, decision making
- Decreased sexual interest; hyposexuality or hypersexuality
- Sleep disturbance (too little, too much, interrupted)
- Crying and tearfulness
- Tendency to sigh
- Fatigue, lethargy
- Lack of strength
- Physical exhaustion
- Feelings of emptiness and/or heaviness
- Psychomotor retardation or agitation

Symptoms Indicative of Anxiety and Hyperarousal

Motor tension
- Trembling, shaking, twitching
- Muscle tension, aches, soreness
- Easy fatigability
- Headache
- Restlessness and searching for something to do

Autonomic hyperactivity
- Anxiety, tension, nervousness
- Heart palpitations, tachycardia
- Shortness of breath
- Numbness, tingling sensations
- Smothering sensations
- Dizziness, unsteady feelings, faintness
- Dry mouth
- Sweating or cold, clammy hands
- Hot flashes or chills
- Chest pain, pressure, discomfort
- Choking
- Nausea, diarrhea, other abdominal distress
- Frequent urination
- Tightness in the throat, trouble swallowing, feeling of something stuck in the throat
- Digestive disturbance

Vigilance and scanning
- Heightened arousal
- Agitation
- Sense of being "geared up"
- Exaggerated startle response
- Irritability, outbursts of anger
- Difficulty falling or staying asleep
- Impaired concentration
- Hypervigilance
- Physiologic reactivity upon exposure to events that symbolize or resemble an aspect of the death or events associated with it

Other Symptoms Indicative of Physiological Response to Distress

In addition to the other physical symptoms already mentioned:
- Hair loss
- Constellation of vague, diffuse somatic complaints, sometimes experienced in waves lasting minutes to hours
- Gastrointestinal symptoms

• Cardiopulmonary symptoms
• Pseudoneurologic symptoms

No definition of grief can be confined to the first part of grief under consideration in this chapter. Whether a person is in the first or last phase of grief, the definition of grief still applies to that last phase, as well as the first. Consequently, in Rando's definition, psychological, behavioral, social, and physical reactions must be included in the understanding of grief from its beginning to its end. The features under them span the entire grief process as well. For example, under the psychological category, affects, or emotions, is one of the four features. Emotions are included in grief from its beginning to its end. However, some of these emotions, such as sorrow, may be experienced before the funeral, whereas others, such as anger, may not emerge for months or even years in some cases. Nor does everyone experience the same emotions in the same sequence, with the same intensity or according to the same timetable.

This variability is true for each of the four kinds of reactions and the many features and content listed under them. Consequently, it would be worse than useless for a pastor to care for a grieving person during the first part of grief based on the assumption that all grieving people experience this or that particular aspect of the initial grief reaction. For this reason, the lists should be seen as containing possible ways grieving people may react to a death, not only from the time when the person learns of the death through the funeral but also through the entire grief process. Some parts of the lists are more likely to be experienced early on during grief, but it would be impossible to pick them out and omit the others. Ministers have the opportunity to choose from the lists according to individual instances of grief.

The Initial Phase of Grief

Because the definition of grief cannot be confined to the initial part of grief, there must be some way of focusing more directly on grief from the point of learning about the death through the funeral. This need for focus provides motivation to approach grief from the standpoint of its stages or phases. Although all phases of grief cannot be coordinated with certain periods, the initial phase quite naturally can be coordinated with the beginning of grief, starting with the point of learning about the death and extending at least through the day of the funeral. This does not mean that once the funeral is over, the mourners are launched into the second phase of the grief process automatically, or that some aspects of the second phase cannot already be manifested before the funeral. Rather, during the few days between learning about the death and waking up on the day following the funeral, bereaved people are just starting out on their journey of grief, and it would hardly make sense to skip over the first phase, which predominates during this time. More importantly, as we will see in a later chapter, the funeral is associated with the initial phases of grief and mourning.

Rando calls the initial phase of grief the avoidance phase, marked by the "understandable desire to avoid the terrible acknowledgment that the loved one is lost" (33). I can identify with this as a pastor. For instance, at the news of hearing about a certain church member's death from one of her good friends who had found her at home earlier in the day, I had a sinking feeling and didn't want it to be true. Though she had been a church member for more years than I had been alive, her sudden death was a real surprise. In her prime, she had been a "mover and shaker" in the congregation and still was very loved. Now I had the onerous task of informing the congregation of her death.

Rando, along with many others, says the avoidance phase of grief consists of shock followed by denial. Her qualification is that she is writing about the avoidance phase as it would apply to "sudden, unexpected death" (30) as opposed to an anticipated death. Because circumstances help determine the response to death to some extent, such qualification can be useful. Nevertheless, this qualification does raise a question about whether the avoidance phase also applies to grief in situations where death was anticipated. In a study of widows, Glick, Weiss, and Parkes affirm that this phase does include situations involving anticipated, as well as unexpected, death. Writing about the first phase of grief, they note: "Shock was reported as regularly by women whose husbands died after an extended illness as by those whose husbands died suddenly, although in the former case the shock was more subdued and tended to stem less from the fact of the death than from the time at which it came" (1974, 53–54).

It will be helpful if ministers distinguish between trauma and shock. Trauma is a reaction to such things as sudden, unexpected tragedies and can devastate a person, a group, a community or even a nation (see chapter 5). Sometimes death is traumatic for survivors, but not always. Shock has been used to describe trauma, but the two need to be separated. This distinction makes it easier to view shock as the initial grief reaction to the death, even though the situation is not traumatic. A person can experience mild shock without being traumatized, or devastated. Shock can be akin to being "taken aback" or "surprised" at the news of a death, as well as being far more intense in devastating circumstances. Nevertheless, be aware that intense bereavement situations have been the measuring stick for describing shock, which will be seen next.

Shock

In the previous discussion about the psychological response, shock and denial are listed as psychological defenses, or attempts at coping. When grief is portrayed as a process, it tends to be described as a series of ways that the human psyche attempts to cope with grief over time. But these efforts to cope are not conscious ways of behaving, such as wearing dark clothes or singing an elegy. Shock provides a good example. If it is intense, it can be akin to someone sneaking up on you and hitting you from behind with a sledgehammer. After being hit, you don't reflect on the way you are going to respond, but instead you are knocked for a loop before you have any time for reflection.

Shock happens at the time when the person learns about the death. *The Oxford English Dictionary* shows that the word *shock* has a history helpful for understanding its meaning in grief. Imagine being a farmer who has a large field of corn (or grain). When it comes time to harvest the corn, you take a certain number of stalks and tie them together. This is called a sheaf. When you have collected sixty sheaves and have bound them together into a large unit, you have a shock. When the shock of corn has sat for the proper length of time to dry and ripen, you carry it to market. In accord with more generalized definitions, *shock* has been applied to many different groupings of things, such as merchandise, plots of land, and financial accounts. Even the military borrowed the word. In its military meaning, the word *shock* signified that an armed force was encountering the enemy in a charge. Now *shock* not only had to do with a grouping of something, in this case a group of soldiers, but it also had the added meaning of engaging an enemy. Increasingly the word took on this meaning of engaging the enemy, while groups of things bunched together dropped out of the meaning. For instance, another military meaning was that two mounted warriors were charging one another. From here, additional generalized meanings of shock have emphasized various kinds of destabilizing or harmful effects on whatever or whoever is receiving a violent blow or clash.

In the twentieth century, *shock* was applied to many areas. As the *Merriam-Webster's Collegiate Dictionary* indicates, now we have culture shock, future shock, shell shock, insulin shock, and many other kinds of shock. It is surprising that in the mid-twentieth century, someone didn't coin the term *grief shock.*

In grief, *shock* means two interrelated things. First, it refers to the blow a person receives upon hearing the news that a family member or friend has died. Receiving the news is the blow. In this regard, it is common to hear phrases like, "The news came as a real shock to me." Second, and more predominately, *shock* refers to the effect of the blow on those who receive it. As mentioned earlier, a person does not have to be completely and utterly traumatized to experience shock, which can be very mild in comparison with extreme trauma, but descriptions tend to emphasize the more extreme instances of shock.

Mostly, descriptions depend on analogies, with *shock* applied to other areas. For instance, Rando writes, "The world is shaken, and the mourner may be overwhelmed" (33). Being shaken is one of the main effects of shock in the physical world, from simple oscillation in which an object starts moving back and forth internally due to a blow, all the way to violent shaking of the earth to due the shock waves of an earthquake. No wonder many descriptions seem to characterize what it is like for the inner world of the bereaved person to be shaken violently. For instance, Lily Pincus, a social worker who started the Institute for Marital Studies at the Tavistock Institute for Human Rights in London, wrote: "All studies agree that *shock* is the first response to the death of an important person, and that shock...may find expression in physical collapse...in violent outbursts...or in dazed withdrawal, denial, and inability to take in the reality of the death" (Pincus, 1974, 112–13).

A second analogy is with the human body going into shock due to trauma. According to Rando, "Like the physical shock that occurs with trauma to the body, the human psyche goes into shock with the traumatic assault of the death of the loved one" (1993, 33). When the human body goes into shock due to severe injury, such as being crushed or burned, there is a "profound depression of vital processes associated with reduced blood volume and pressure" (*Merriam-Webster's Collegiate Dictionary*). Likewise, when a grieving person goes "into shock," there is a "profound depression of vital processes."

One of the main vital processes that may shut down temporarily is emotion: "Emotionally, the mourner may become numb" (Rando, 1993, 33), temporarily having no emotional reaction to the news of death. Numbness, or becoming devoid of feeling, is not necessarily a bad thing during shock. Glick, Weiss, and Parkes report that when widows who were told of their husband's death felt nothing at first, it was viewed as a blessing:

> Frequently they said that when they were told that their husband was no longer alive they were surprised to notice that they were devoid of any feeling. Later they usually felt that numbness at that moment had been a blessing, preferable to the pain that they were not sure they were then ready to bear. (1974, 53)

Another vital process that may shut down temporarily is comprehension. Along with Pincus and others, Rando says, "It is not uncommon for the individual to feel confused, dazed, bewildered, and unable to comprehend what has happened" (1993, 33). Lacking comprehension, the person experiences disbelief in conjunction with numbness. In disbelief, the bereaved temporarily cannot comprehend that a loved one really is dead (see Glick, Weiss, and Parkes, 1974, 54–56).

One Sunday afternoon, a pastor walked into a hospital room to visit an elderly church member, a woman who had been physically declining for several years and was trying to recover from a serious illness. As she entered the room, the pastor encountered both adult children of the sick church member, along with their spouses and three children. One couple belonged to the pastor's church, but the other couple and their three children were members in another denomination. Immediately, the pastor recognized everyone present, because just four months ago she had conducted the funeral of the sick woman's husband. As she approached the bed, one of the adult children told her what she now could see for herself. The elderly church member had died just a few minutes before the pastor entered the room. She was jarred, or shaken, as she looked at the body and then at each person standing around the bed. The shock was subdued and relatively mild, but it was present nevertheless, in everyone including the pastor. Adults and children alike looked as if nothing had happened, as if they were numb and uncomprehending, or comprehending only in the most shallow way. This seemed to be confirmed in the awkward and shallow politeness of their voices when the pastor, also feeling awkward as she tried to gather her wits about her, expressed her sorrow over the loss.

But shock, with its numbness, disbelief, and confusion, starts wearing off, sometimes quickly, sometimes more gradually. The next day, when the pastor met with the family, the impact of the loss was more evident, though the full measure of pain and sorrow would emerge only over time. Presently, the second part of the avoidance phase of grief was taking effect. According to Rando, as recognition of the death is slowly let into conscious awareness, shock begins receding. Right away, another buffer protecting the bereaved against the full impact of pain emerges, called denial.

Denial

You may be familiar with denial from having read Elizabeth Kübler-Ross's famous book, *On Death and Dying,* in which she identifies denial, along with isolation, as the first stage of a terminally ill patient's reaction to receiving the bad news of impending death (1969, 38). Or, you may have heard or read about denial in alcoholism and other addictions. Psychotherapist Nancy McWilliams gives several examples of denial:

> Spouses who deny that their abusive partner is dangerous, alcoholics who insist that they have no drinking problem, mothers who ignore the evidence of sexual molestation of their daughters, elderly people who will not consider giving up a driver's license despite obvious impairment–all are familiar examples of denial at its worst. (1994, 102)

Denial, says *Merriam-Webster's,* is "a psychological defense mechanism in which confrontation with a personal problem or with reality is avoided by denying the existence of the problem or reality." According to

McWilliams, this rejection of reality is an "instant, nonrational process" (1994, 98) as opposed to being the result of a conscious decision to forget about something because it is too painful.

In grief, denial is not a complete and utter disavowal of the death itself, but instead it is a partial denial enabling the bereaved person to begin absorbing the news of death at a pace that can be handled. Along with awareness comes pain, so denial also acts as an "emotional anesthesia" (Rando, 1993, 33), or a kind of emotional painkiller, manifested through such things as forgetting about the death momentarily.

This anesthesia, too, is partial, because there can be an abundance of emotional pain during the initial phase of grief. Glick, Weiss, and Parkes, in their study of widows, say that as shock and disbelief began receding, "the widows' underlying feelings of almost all-encompassing sorrow emerged to be expressed in sadness and in weeping and crying" (1974, 56). More generally, for males and females, and for young and old alike, there can be a variety of emotional reactions: "From some, there may be outbursts of emotion—anger, intense sorrow and sadness, hysteria, tears, rageful protest, screaming" (Rando, 1993, 33). Not everyone, however, tends to go in this direction: "From others, there may be quiet withdrawal or mechanical action without feeling. Some report feeling depersonalized, as if they were witnessing the experience happening to someone else" (33).

In her quote above, McWilliams gave negative examples of denial. However, denial also can play a positive role in a person's life. For instance:

> In crises or emergencies, a capacity to deny emotionally that one's survival is at risk can be lifesaving: One can take the most realistically effective and even heroic actions using denial. Every war brings tales of people who "kept their heads" in terrifying, life-threatening conditions, and saved themselves and their fellows. (1994, 102)

Likewise, in the avoidance phase of grief, denial plays a positive role during the time leading up to the funeral. It is a shame that so many works on grief mention no examples other than the most gut-wrenching kind, in which the bereaved person is portrayed as almost completely debilitated, if they mention any examples at all. There are untold numbers of instances when the bereaved are able to do what needs to be done quite courageously and effectively. They play host to relatives and endure family tensions. They deal with supportive family and friends who surround them. They make difficult decisions at the funeral home. They talk to the pastor about the funeral. They make financial decisions and search for legal documents. They spend hour upon hour at the visitation. They face the day of the funeral. They do these things and more, with varying degrees of difficulty and pain, against a background of denial, which enables them to accomplish what has to be done. Lily

Pincus calls this time between the initial shock and the funeral a "controlled phase" (1974, 115).

Ministers may experience denial as well during this time. Sometimes, the minister has no personal connection to the deceased or to the family, and grief certainly should not be feigned. Families and friends often appreciate the fact that the pastor may be preaching a funeral sermon without having known the dead loved one. Yet, there also can be numerous times when the minister did have a meaningful relationship with a church member who died. In these instances, the minister is no more exempt from grief than anyone else and may be operating out of a low level of shock followed by partial denial.

With its buffering effect, denial helps the minister accomplish difficult tasks, just as it helps family members. For instance, calling on a bereaved widow or widower is not an easy thing to do, especially if you are attempting to make the death seem real, too. Nor is preparing the funeral a casual matter done in an offhand way. Every step of the way, reflection involving the deceased, loved ones of the deceased, and other church members and friends plays a role in funeral preparation. A story from your relationship with the deceased finds its way into the sermon. A prayer is written as you think about how the children of the deceased are holding up. You include a passage of scripture that you had discussed with the deceased only a few weeks ago in a class. Grief from some past death begins to be stirred up in you.

Without denial, a minister would have a much more difficult time interacting with the bereaved, preparing funerals and conducting them, while also rescheduling meetings and getting ready for next Sunday. But it is important to realize that this is not a negative, unhealthy thing, unless it becomes a way of life (see chapter 11). Instead, it is a natural part of the grief process for the minister, just as it is for others. This means that against the background of denial serving as a buffer, ministers too have the pain of sorrow. They become sad. They weep, and sometimes they may even want to scream in outrage. Conversely, they may have a sense of unreality or find themselves going about their business in a mechanical way, as if they were immune from death and grief. So, in many instances, the minister is one of the mourners who just happens to be the one conducting the funeral.

Causes of Variation in the Initial Phase of Grief

In the context of discussing pastoral care with a newly bereaved person, minister John Mansell writes: "I first thought that the circumstances around the death largely shaped the manner in which the bereaved experienced their grief. While such considerations do contribute to a degree when a person experiences loss, I have found that death is death. Regardless of the circumstances, death is painful" (1998,

14–15). This statement reminds me of a particular funeral experience that really brought home to me that "death is death." I received a phone call from a local funeral director who asked me if I would do a funeral for the family of a man who had died. He was very elderly. He had no church, no spouse, and only a few living relatives, but they lived in other cities. There were a handful of family members coming to the funeral from out of town, but they just wanted a very brief ceremony, as little as ten or fifteen minutes. I agreed to do the funeral, but I would not be meeting the family until the day of the funeral, during the brief visitation right before the funeral service. For some reason, I had gotten the impression from the funeral director that the family members were more or less just doing their family duty by having the funeral. Perhaps it was their desire to have such a short funeral ceremony that conveyed this. I arrived at the funeral home expecting the whole thing to be rather perfunctory, but I was surprised by the touching displays of grief shown by family members. It mattered not that they had lived far away for many years. One of their beloved family members was dead, and it brought them real pain. This experience taught me a lesson: Do not make assumptions about the grief of relatives, or of anyone, based on the external appearance of a situation. Death is indeed death, and it does bring pain.

Rando deals with this from a different angle. She argues that the factors associated with a death combine to help make the grief of those who mourn a unique experience. As she puts it, grief is "influenced, shaped, and determined by a constellation of factors that combine to render a mourner's response unique–as individual as a fingerprint" (1993, 29). She names a host of these factors and places them under three broad categories, including psychological factors, social factors, and physiological factors. These factors are presented below so that you can refer to them in your care of the bereaved. There are two things to remember, however. First, the lists below apply also to grief beyond the funeral and first phase of grief. Second, the lists should be used neither to stereotype any grieving person, nor to give you a false sense of knowledge about grieving people for whom you care.

PSYCHOLOGICAL FACTORS

(quoted from Rando, 1993, 31–32; also see Rando, 1984)

Characteristics Pertaining to the Nature and Meaning of the Specific Loss

- The unique nature and meaning of the loss sustained or relationship severed
- Qualities of the relationship lost (psychological character, strength, and security of the attachment)

- Roles the deceased occupied in the mourner's family or social system (number of roles, functions served, their centrality and importance)
- Characteristics of the deceased
- Amount of unfinished business between the mourner and the deceased
- Mourner's perception of the deceased's fulfillment in life
- Number, type, and quality of secondary losses
- Nature of any ongoing relationship with the deceased

Characteristics of the Mourner

- Coping behaviors, personality, and mental health
- Level of maturity and intelligence
- Assumptive world
- Previous life experiences, especially past experiences with loss and death
- Expectations about grief and mourning
- Social, cultural, ethnic, generational, and religious/philosophical/spiritual background
- Sex-role conditioning
- Age
- Developmental stages of life, lifestyle, and sense of meaning and fulfillment
- Presence of concurrent stresses or crises

Characteristics of the Death

- The death surround (location, type of death, reasons for it, mourner's presence at it, degree of confirmation of it, mourner's degree of preparation and participation)
- Timeliness
- Psychosocial context within which the death occurs
- Amount of mourner's anticipation of the death
- Degree of suddenness
- Mourner's perception of preventability
- Length of illness prior to the death
- Amount, type, and quality of anticipatory grief and involvement with the dying person

SOCIAL FACTORS

(quoted from Rando, 1993, 31–32)

- Mourner's social support system and the recognition, validation, acceptance, and assistance provided by its members

- Mourner's social, cultural, ethnic, generational, and
  religious/philosophical/spiritual background
- Mourner's educational, economic, and occupational status
- Funerary or memorial rites
- Involvement in the legal system
- Amount of time since the death

PHYSIOLOGICAL FACTORS

(quoted from Rando, 1993, 31–32)

- Drugs (including alcohol, caffeine, and nicotine)
- Nutrition
- Rest and sleep
- Exercise
- Physical health

One erroneous use of this list would be to assume that by identifying the "constellation of factors" surrounding the death, you could make stereotyping inferences from this constellation about the grief experience of the bereaved. For instance, if a person who has been battling cancer for five years finally succumbs, a stereotyping assumption would be that the loving family members may be expected to manifest the same configuration of features from the lists above as everyone else who has that circumstance. Such stereotyping can cause those who care for the bereaved to miss the actual pain of grief, as Mansell discovered.

Instead, knowing the constellation of factors should help reveal the unique grief experience of the bereaved. If, for instance, I had known more about the relationship of the elderly man to the family members who attended his funeral, I would have been more open to the possibility that the funeral was going to be an important and meaningful experience for them. Yet, the reality is that pastors often operate on the basis of very partial knowledge of the constellation of factors surrounding a death and contributing to individuality in grief. So the wisest course of action seems to be on the one hand to keep your eyes and ears open to discerning the constellation of factors, while on the other hand remembering always that death is death. Approach those who mourn with an attitude of openness to their unique experience, which may be "as individual as a fingerprint."

Finally, even though pastors often know only some factors contributing to variation in grief, they nevertheless may find themselves in a very strategic position to gather knowledge of the constellation of factors surrounding a death in some instances. Many times, ministers are involved with church members who die, and they know their family and some of their friends, at least those in the congregation. In this respect, they sometimes can be way ahead of psychotherapists who must begin putting together the story of grief through diagnostic interviews months or years after the fact. Daily life in pastoral ministry inherently provides pastors with knowledge and relationships that become the ground of effective care before and during funerals and may provide the basis of effective care during the months and years following the funeral. Consequently, those who do not participate in a church, but who, so to speak, seek a minister from the yellow pages for a funeral, potentially are depriving themselves not only of good pastoral care but also of a supportive community of loving and caring people who will not be going away after the funeral.

Conclusion

There is quite a bit for pastors to know about grief as it is experienced before and during funerals. As Rando's definition of grief shows, grief is manifested in a variety of ways, psychologically, behaviorally, socially, and physically. In the avoidance phase of grief, those who grieve experience shock and denial. This enables bereaved people not only to experience pain in doses that can be tolerated at the beginning of the grief process, but also it helps them do the things that need to be done before and during the funeral. Finally, the grief of real, live people cannot be stereotyped, but has uniqueness flowing from the combination of factors associated with the death being mourned.

CHAPTER FOUR

Caring for Individuals and Families Who Mourn

Now that the beginning of grief has been discussed, it is time to consider those who will be attending the funeral. As we saw in chapter 2, mourners are those who attend a funeral out of respect or affection for the deceased. Each person at the funeral can be called a mourner, and all the people at the funeral, the group as a whole, can be called mourners. In this chapter, individuals who mourn and families who mourn will be discussed, and caring for them in pastoral ministry will be addressed. In the next chapter, mourners who are not family members will be discussed.

A Funeral Story

If your experience is anything like mine, you probably have not focused much, or at all, on funerals in seminary. In any case, your funeral education may take off like a spaceship going into warp speed when you get out of school and into your first church, where you are confronted with your first funeral as an ordained minister. I was lucky. My first church was in an area where two, or sometimes even three, ministers commonly participated in the same funeral due to family requests. So I went through at least two or three funerals before I had to conduct one by myself. In those early days of my ministry, I was learning how to conduct funerals out of necessity, and I experienced how the funeral brings those who mourn together.

One funeral will forever stand out in my mind. It was near the end of my first year in pastoral ministry. Early one morning I was putting gas in the car, preparing to drive to a meeting, when a church member drove up, got out of his car, and told me that another church member had committed suicide earlier that morning. Of course, I was stunned.

Operating on instinct, I paid for the gas and drove to the home of the dead church member immediately. This man had been a highly respected member of the church and a well-known business leader in the surrounding area. I arrived at the house and knocked on the door expecting to find his wife, along with his three young adult children who lived in different communities not too far away. However, when I entered the living room I encountered what seemed like half the church members sitting around the room in a huge circle along with the wife and children of the deceased man. After sorrowful greetings and being told what had happened, I sat down and almost immediately was asked to say a prayer. When I finished praying, the group began to disperse.

I hardly remember the next few days before the funeral. I do remember the wife's request that a former minister of the church preach the funeral sermon. This was not very surprising because she sometimes had spoken of this minister in the most glowing terms, as if he were a beloved family friend. I also recall receiving phone calls from a colleague or two and from various business people from around the area who expressed condolences and support.

The visitation was at a large funeral home in a nearby town, where the funeral was to take place the next morning. Of the few funerals I had conducted, this was the largest by a wide margin. Naturally, the family was present, including the elderly parents of the deceased, his widow, his children, and various other family members from out of town. Many church members were there, people who had known the deceased for many years. There were others present from the community whom I knew, and there were many who were strangers to me. Everything was going according to plan, but when it came to the funeral sermon, I experienced a kind of letdown. The former minister had received such a buildup that I expected something exceptional. As it turned out, he was rather soft-spoken and brief in his sermon, competent yet unremarkable, at least in my memory. I will resist the temptation to begin analyzing this, except to say that today, many years later, I would understand to a far greater degree the position in which he was being placed. He treated me respectfully, and his behavior and funeral participation were very appropriate.

I wish I could share with you some great pastoral care conversation I had with the wife before the funeral, and how that contributed to my funeral planning. But the truth is that several things worked against this occurring, though we did talk. I had very little experience of death in my own family life on which to draw, too little knowledge of grief and suicide, and too little time as the minister of that church or as a minister at all, to be terribly effective in the realm of caring for the woman or her family, except to go through the situation with them and try to do my best in the funeral. In addition, no one had ever mentioned to me that I would be going through the situation with the congregation and community as well and doing my best in the funeral for numerous people who had an endearing tie, as the dictionary puts it, to the one who died. Today I could fill the rest of this chapter with questions, analysis, imaginings, critique, feelings, and thoughts about that situation, even though it was years ago. When it was happening, we were all in shock and just trying to find our way. When I say that we were in shock, I do not mean just the immediate family members and me, but the entire congregation, much of the local community, and people in nearby communities for miles around. (The next chapter will show that the congregation and community were traumatized.)

During the time before the funeral, and for a brief period after it, I had more contact with the young adult children of the deceased man than I ever had before. They had grown up in the church but none attended it now, except on rare occasions. One of the children tried to take over the family business following the funeral, but he could not keep it alive any more than his father could save it. The business was being victimized by changing times and a nationwide economic downturn over which neither father nor son had any control whatsoever. Some people in the community presumed that the father had committed suicide because his business was about to go under. Years ago, he had taken over the business from his father, who still lived in the community. This puts us in the realm of shame, depression, and who knows what family pressures, and it leads us to ponder the motivation driving the son to try to save the family business. Most of all, it makes us wonder about the pain, not only the pain of the father who killed himself, but also about the pain of the family members who survived it, pain that went beyond that of all the other hundreds of people who were grieving his loss.

One night around 9:00, a few weeks after the funeral, the entire community received a stark symbol revealing the family's pain, and that of the church and community as well. I was returning home and was about a mile outside the little community in which I lived when I noticed a glow on the other side of a hill just ahead. When I topped the hill, I saw fire reaching into the night sky. The big wood frame building housing the family business was burning. Rumors circulated that a family member had set fire to the building in order to get the insurance money, but for all I know, it was purely accidental. However it started, to me the fire always had tremendous symbolic meaning. For a long time, I saw it as representing anger of the family members. Over the years, as I have learned more about the suffering that grief and suicide bring to people, I have come to see that the fire represented much more than any run-of-the-mill anger. It expressed the depths of the soul. Its intense heat radiated utter rage. Its glowing sparks floating into the darkness were like pieces of grieving selves that had been suddenly shattered and carried away in the wind. Its light shined forth the devastation of the spouse, the children, the parents, and other family members and friends. The shell of a building left in its wake showed the brokenness sitting right there in the middle of the community, so that no one could hide from the reality of death and destruction.

One effect the suicide had on the congregation was that the congregation developed a quality I can only describe as brittleness, which was experienced in worship, as well as more generally in fellowship. This experience went on for six months, until we decided to do something about it. It was time to plan for a traditional, annual event in the church that was a holdover from times past. This week consisted of nightly worship services featuring a guest preacher. This year, we invited a minister known for his preaching ability and asked him to address our collective grief. When I talked to him about this, he responded that he had a sermon series on Job and that he would be willing to come for the week. He was an intellectual and serious-minded person whose sermons tended to be on the weighty side. His style was straightforward. He did not warm up the congregation with stupid chatter or jokes, but instead he just said what he had to say. On the first night, the sanctuary was filled, including some people who normally would not be caught dead in the church. I wondered how attendance would hold up during the course of the week, and frankly I was a little surprised that it remained steady.

I had not known what to expect, really, because I had no experience with this sort of thing. All I can say is that the week turned out to be just what the doctor ordered. Following this week of worship services, the brittleness went away. The congregation returned to its sense of life, and I had the feeling that we could move on in our life together.

Caring for Individuals Who Mourn

If you had to choose one person in the story above with whom you were going to practice pastoral care, who would it be? The wife of the deceased is an obvious choice; let's stay with her for a moment. If you were going to care for her, how would you proceed? Probably, you would go to her house to see her as soon as you got word of the death, like I did. Then you would make an appointment to talk to her, and other family members, about the funeral. Finally, you would be at the visitation and would conduct the funeral, realizing that she, and her family, would be a central part of it. These things would be typical and would fit with the traditional pastoral care and counseling approach to caring for the bereaved, at least from the point of death through the funeral.

Paul Irion's book *The Funeral and the Mourners: Pastoral Care of the Bereaved* (1954) contains the rudimentary beginnings of what became the pastoral care and counseling approach to caring for bereaved individuals before, during, and after funerals. Irion viewed the funeral from the psychological, theological, social, cultural, and aesthetic perspectives. From the standpoint of the psychological perspective, the mourners are seen as individuals, as opposed to being seen as a group: "When we approach the funeral in its psychological dimension, we immediately become aware of the necessity for dealing with mourners as individuals" (Irion, 1954, 41). At this point, no particular mourner is singled out as the bereaved individual, such as a family member of the deceased. Rather, it could be anyone, or everyone, who grieves and attends the funeral, because the psychological perspective is used for discussing a certain dimension of the funeral.

However, approaching the funeral "in its psychological dimension" (or other perspectives) does not stand alone in pastoral care and counseling. In addition, pre-funeral encounters between the minister and bereaved individual, the funeral, and post-funeral encounters are approached from the standpoint of pastoral counseling. In this perspective, the funeral is placed in the middle of a series, which begins at the point of death, includes the time from the point of death up to the funeral, then moves to the funeral itself, and concludes with the time following the funeral that stretches through the grief process. Unlike the psychological perspective on the funeral, which does not require identifying specific people, pastoral care and counseling does require a focus on specific individuals. According to Irion, "The ministry to the dying, the prefuneral calls, the funeral itself are in reality precounseling contacts with the bereaved. They pave the way for a more continuous and well-structured counseling relationship after the funeral" (1954, 159; also see 19).

This counseling relationship is with a specific, identified person. The concept of pre-counseling comes from Seward Hiltner's book *Pastoral Counseling* (1949), in which Hiltner attempted to show how different aspects of ministry could lead to pastoral counseling. Any part of ministry, including a funeral, could be termed pre-counseling when viewed from the standpoint of how it might lead to pastoral counseling.

This traditional approach, if we begin at the point of death, first involves pre-funeral calling, in which the minister practices pastoral care by visiting a newly bereaved church member, as well as any other family members or friends who are present. Ideally, the minister schedules a second meeting, which includes the family, for funeral planning and remembering the deceased. This second meeting is not a counseling conversation, but it can be seen as part of caring for the bereaved in the sense that it certainly does relate to their grief. Meeting with the family members when they arrive at the visitation to view the body provides a third instance of pre-funeral care.

Depending on circumstances, there may be only one conversation, in which the focus shifts back and forth between care and planning. But, whether there are one or two conversations, during this pre-funeral contact between the minister and bereaved individual (and other family members), the minister actually is looking beyond the funeral to post-funeral pastoral counseling in the sense that the ground for the pastoral counseling already is being prepared, as the person experiences the beginnings of the grief process.

Next comes the funeral, seen from the standpoint of facilitating, as opposed to inhibiting, the grief of the bereaved person. This is further preparation for the pastoral counseling.

Following the funeral, the minister and bereaved individual begin a series of post-funeral pastoral counseling sessions focusing on the person's grief process. This has been described as occurring within the context of pastoral visitation over a period of weeks, and potentially months, and within support groups (for instance, see Switzer, 1974, 155–67, and 2000, 114–16).

The first two parts of this movement basically fit what occurs in pastoral ministry, though not completely, as we will see below. However, post-funeral pastoral counseling in the context of visitation lasting for weeks or months has never fit pastoral ministry. This approach can address neither the vast amount of grief in many churches, nor the actual long-term course of the grief process, often lasting well over a year. In addition, for every grieving church member who attends a support group, dozens more never will.

Assume for the sake of argument that I was attempting to care for the widow of the man who committed suicide by following the pastoral care and counseling model. I started out appropriately, going to visit her as soon as I learned of the death. But right away I ran into a complication, as the room was filled with church members. In that living room, I found myself in a very public situation, caring through the ministry of presence and prayer for the widow, for the young adult children, and for the rest of the people there all at the same time. My sense of being in a public situation combined with my experience of ministering to the group as a whole in the living room seemed more similar to a funeral than to a private conversation between the widow and me. Furthermore, the presence of church members there demonstrates a fairly complex situation. On the one hand, lay care was happening before I arrived, showing the fallacy of believing that the ordained minister alone practices pastoral care. On the other hand, these church members were grieving too, showing that the minister's care of the bereaved cannot be confined to a spouse or other family members.

Actually, in my first year of ministry, it never would have occurred to me to view this initial visit with the bereaved as pre-counseling. It was hard enough to think ahead to the funeral, much less beyond the funeral to what might be happening weeks later. I was just trying to get through the day. Now, many years later, I find looking toward the funeral and beyond it much easier due to experience, but I still do not think of caring encounters with mourners before the funeral as pre-counseling. Nor do I think of the funeral as pre-counseling. Instead, I find it far more helpful to view all my encounters with mourners before the funeral, including pastoral care conversations, as part of a movement culminating in the funeral. The funeral is the most important means of caring for the bereaved during the initial phase of grief, and for this reason I believe that it must be seen as a form of caring for the bereaved in its own right, regardless of what happens after it. In no way does this mean that pastoral care ends following the funeral, but it does mean that the funeral is not merely a prelude to counseling.

Limits to Caring for Individuals Who Mourn

In actual practice, individuals who most often reap the benefit of pre-funeral pastoral care are the ones responsible for making funeral arrangements, usually family members whom the minister visits after receiving a call from the funeral home. One benefit is that it may help the bereaved person begin dealing with grief, but many times the minister is having the experience of encountering the grief that has begun quite independently of the initial pastoral care visit. To complicate matters, a person may not begin experiencing their grief, in the sense of feeling emotion, for several days, perhaps at the funeral or at the burial, or some time after that.

Another benefit of pre-funeral pastoral care is that it gives the minister and person a connection they would not have otherwise going into the funeral. The point here is not that they are strangers before the death occurred, unless the person is not a church member. They may know each other quite well. Instead, they broach the issues of death and grief together. This affects not only the minister's funeral planning, but also how they may experience each other in the funeral, as well as affecting the impact the funeral may have on the person. So pre-funeral pastoral care with those making funeral arrangements must be strongly affirmed in pastoral ministry.

However, that is only part of the story, as it was when I entered the living room of the widow on the morning of her husband's death. It is what lies beyond the expected and necessary pre-funeral pastoral care with family members who are making funeral arrangements that reveals the limits of caring for individuals who mourn.

First Limitation: Time and Numbers

Most of the people who attend funerals have no pastoral care with the minister before the funeral. They neither reap its benefit nor contribute to funeral planning. Yet, they attend the funeral. It would be a physical impossibility for the minister to care for every mourner individually, so caring for individuals before the funeral may be only for the few. This is not to take away the importance of caring for a grieving family member who is making funeral arrangements. It simply points to a limit of caring for individuals before funerals in pastoral ministry.

Keep in mind that lay care by organized groups in the church, and the mutual care of members, should be included in the understanding of pastoral care at this time, and the minister should never think that there is no care other than that in which the ordained minister is involved. However, the focus in this chapter is on the minister, with the funeral in mind.

Second Limitation: Family and Other Mourners

In pastoral care and counseling, the focus in the funeral tends to remain on an individual family member who received pre-funeral pastoral care and who will be visited after the funeral by the minister. Everyone else at the funeral tends to be characterized as a group of people who support the grieving family member through their attendance. This view of non-family mourners, and even other family members, is extremely common throughout the literature on the psychological understanding of grief. The problem with it is that non-family mourners grieve, too.

This is a tricky issue, because there is a distinction between the family members and everyone else at the funeral. The family members lost a loved one and grieve at a level beyond what others may be experiencing, though there are exceptions and complications depending on circumstances. Moreover, the death typically will affect them more profoundly than it will others during the months and years ahead. They deserve to be supported as the grieving family members.

At the same time, however, other mourners grieve also, which means that they do not experience attending the funeral solely as a supportive act, but also as something for themselves in their grief. Indeed, support itself can be part of mourning in the sense of being a customary expression of grief. A young woman in her early twenties was at her father's funeral when she noticed several strangers there who had introduced themselves to her during the visitation on the previous evening. These were people who had worked with her father, and the young woman had assumed that they were being respectful by attending the visitation. Now, however, when she saw them at the funeral, she realized that they too were bereaved over the loss of her father, their colleague.

If you are the minister conducting the funeral, undoubtedly you will recognize the distinction between family members and other mourners, but simultaneously you will recognize that others also grieve. Caring for individuals who mourn must be seen as part of a larger whole, in which the funeral is a form of caring for all who mourn, including family members, church members, other known friends, and strangers.

Third Limitation: Connections and Context

Notice how hard it is to be specific about the bereaved individual receiving pastoral care without mentioning the family of the deceased. In spite of the nearly exclusive focus on the individual in the psychological understanding of grief, the family often is included in grief and funeral discussions. Increasingly, "the family" may be discussed in place of "the individual," and even plugged into the same expected pre-funeral, funeral and post-funeral care previously discussed in terms of the grieving individual (see, for instance, Oates, 1997, 26–29).

In reality, ministers often care for individuals in the context of caring for the immediate family, family of origin, extended family, or close friends depending on circumstances. The family does not remain a generalized family, merely providing context for the individual. Nor does the individual disappear when the family as a whole is being addressed in pastoral care. Instead, within the family, the minister may deal with couples, children, teenagers, and adults of all ages. Some family members are in-laws, who may be distinguished from blood relatives at this time more than any other. Some family members may be well known to the minister, and others may be strangers. Some may be church members, and others may be members of neighboring churches (see Capps, 2001, for a helpful discussion of the individual in the family system).

Caring for Families Who Mourn

Because the minister traditionally meets with the family to discuss the funeral, it is an opportunity to reminisce about the deceased (see Mansell, 1998, 16–23, on leading this discussion). Although this often happens naturally among the bereaved, it has been emphasized as an important aspect of grieving in pastoral care and counseling, based on the writings of Freud and Lindemann (see Irion, 1966, 102–3). Anderson and Foley emphasize the importance of such storytelling for grieving in their book, *Mighty Stories, Dangerous Rituals: Weaving Together the Human and the Divine* (1998). Storytelling about the deceased helps the bereaved "make a memory" (112), which they view as the central purpose of grieving. "Effecting the transition from relating to a living presence to building an enduring memory is the work of grieving" (113).

They go on to point out that "The first stories told by grievers do not provide a definitive interpretation of the life of the deceased. They are rather scattered recollections of the deceased that eventually will be revised again and again through the process of forming a narrative" (112).

If the initial stories told by those who grieve tend to be "scattered recollections" rather than finished products, so the minister's pre-funeral encounters with bereaved families also can seem somewhat scattered and unfinished. The minister's actual experience of the family, and the family members' experience of each other, can be quite varied, which is seen in the cases discussed next.

Adult Children

One common funeral experience in pastoral ministry involves caring for an adult child of the deceased, who has taken on the primary responsibility for making funeral arrangements. If the spouse of the deceased parent is still alive, the adult child may act as an advocate of the surviving parent, making sure things get done. The adult child arrives in the community after a long flight or drive, sometimes days after the death happened. There may be brothers or sisters, but they end up assisting their sibling, even if they live nearby. Of course, the opposite situation can happen also, in which the one who lives nearby can take charge.

Adult children who take on this responsibility may appear to be quite stressed as they juggle several things. Their personal grief may appear to be on hold in public, while they attend to their surviving parent and host other relatives who have just arrived. They may have only a limited time before they have to be back at their job. If they have a family, their family may have come on the trip with them, or the family may be coming later, or not at all.

Many adult children have not been through this sort of experience before, and they become quite anxious when they have to make funeral plans. One such person was so anxious that she could not make decisions without many repetitive phone calls to the funeral director and to the minister. Others do not know the local funeral customs and want to reinvent the wheel, but not in a meaningful or creative way. Once in a great while, the adult child may be exceptionally hostile. I actually received a phone call about this once from a funeral director with whom I had developed a relationship. He needed someone to listen as he lamented having to deal with this person who seemed so coldhearted and uncooperative.

Some adult children are overly controlling, as one minister experienced firsthand. A woman named Margaret, age eighty-four, became a church member three years before her death. Her nephew, Matthew, had invited her to attend the church when she returned from living in another city for many years. Margaret died on a Wednesday and was cremated. A memorial service was scheduled for the following Monday at the church, and burial of the ashes was scheduled for Tuesday morning at a rural cemetery an hour's drive from the church, where many family members were buried, including Margaret's husband.

When Margaret died, the minister, Joan Martin, visited Matthew and his wife, Ruth. But Margaret's daughter, Judith, wanted to plan the memorial service, so Matthew and Ruth were left out of the process.

Judith, who lived in another city, was an only child. She was in her forties, divorced, and was a talented artist. She arrived on Saturday and called Rev. Martin, who proceeded to do something that she quickly regretted. For reasons that seemed good to her at the time, she invited Judith to her house on Sunday afternoon for the memorial service planning session. However, she experienced Judith to be "temperamental, perfectionistic, high-strung and overbearing."

Judith was very particular and went over the whole service with Rev. Martin step by step. For instance, rather than suggesting a favorite hymn, she went through the entire hymnal with her, looking for just the right music. The discussion lasted almost two hours, and to top it off, Judith called a foreign city on the minister's home phone to talk to her boyfriend, who was traveling, telling him about the death and service.

Judith spoke about her mother at the memorial service, and professional musicians played. Rev. Martin also said something about Margaret in her sermon that, as it turned out, was to have significance at the burial. She said that her visits with Margaret usually lasted longer than she planned, because Margaret always had another story to tell.

On Tuesday, approximately thirty people, mostly relatives who had come from around the state, gathered at the cemetery. It was a clear, crisp fall morning. As Judith wished, after Rev. Martin said the words of committal with some poetry added, the two of them lifted the wood box containing the ashes over the grave, a hole one foot square and five feet deep. They held the box at the top of the hole and let go. It fell the five feet and went thump.

Then Judith said to Rev. Martin, "Is that all?"

Wearily, Rev. Martin responded, "Yes, I've done pretty much everything I know how to do." After three days, she had pretty much had it with Judith, for whom she sensed she could not possibly do a good enough job.

Then Judith burst into tears, saying, "This is all wrong."

"What exactly is wrong?" said Rev. Martin.

Judith said, "The hole is in the wrong place. It's not next to my father's grave. It's at the wrong corner of the plot."

Without hesitation, Rev. Martin replied, "We can do something about that."

They called the funeral director over and told him the hole was in the wrong place. He informed the cemetery workers, who were waiting to fill in the grave, and they called their boss, another local funeral director. When he arrived, the two funeral directors "duked it out" about whose fault it was before settling on a course of action. They suggested Judith and the other mourners go back to town and return when the right grave was ready, but she announced that she could not leave until the ashes were in the right place.

It took twenty minutes for the cemetery workers to dig a new grave in the right place. But when they tried to get the ashes out of the wrong grave, they could not do it. They got a crow bar and tried to pry it out, but that did not work. Finally, they dug a hole alongside the grave, came at the box from the side, and retrieved it. This took another forty-five minutes. During this time, Rev. Martin observed one of the cousins taking pictures of the whole thing and thought, "Great, we've got a photographic record of the worst day of my life." Finally, the box containing the ashes was placed by the new grave, and the mourners gathered for a second try at the burial.

"Shouldn't we say something?" said Judith.

"What would you like to say?" said Rev. Martin.

Judith said, "Do you know the book by Judith Viorst called *Ten Good Things About Barney*?"

"Yes, I do know the book," she replied.

This is a children's book about a cat named Barney. After Barney dies, the family gathers around him and says ten good things about him. Judith wanted the group to stand around the right grave and say ten good things about her dead mother. So that's what they did. They mentioned her adventuresome spirit and recalled her great storytelling. They speculated that she would have liked the story of her own burial, and they concluded that what had happened was just right because it fit her.

After the group finished saying ten good things about Margaret, Judith echoed what Rev. Martin had said in her sermon, as she commented, "You see, she's done it again. We've all stayed here much longer than we intended, and we have one more story to tell." Everyone laughed. Then they said the Lord's Prayer, and Rev. Martin and Judith put the box in the right grave. This ceremony seemed very meaningful to Judith and the others.

When it was time to return home, Rev. Martin rode with Matthew, Ruth, and a church member who was a longtime friend of Margaret. This church member had invited her to ride to the cemetery with them. When the church finally was in sight, Rev. Martin thought to herself, "I've made it! I'm home free!" But the day was not quite over.

At that moment, the church member who was driving said, "The only thing that will redeem this day is lunch at my favorite restaurant. I'm going to take you all to lunch." So they drove right past the church and had lunch at the restaurant. After lunch, they dropped Rev. Martin off at the church and drove away. She was so glad to be back that she knelt and kissed the ground.

Black Sheep

Though a real sheep with black wool is relatively rare, many families have a member who gets labeled a black sheep. For instance, a man and woman had been divorced for a decade. He remarried, but she remained single. Eventually she was diagnosed with cancer and died after a struggle lasting several years. Her two daughters, who were in their twenties, took charge of the funeral arrangements and called the minister of the church they attended as a family when they were children. The present minister knew of the mother's cancer and had attempted to visit her because she had remained in the community, but she wanted no contact. The minister also had spoken to her ex-husband on a previous occasion. Because everyone but the mother lived in different cities, and none of them participated in a church community, the daughters returned to their old family church for the funeral.

The black sheep in this family was the ex-husband, the young women's father. They neither wanted him to participate in funeral planning, nor sit with the family at the funeral. He did attend with his present wife, but played no family role at the funeral. Perhaps this could have been a time of reconciliation, but instead it was a time when alienation was reinforced, which sadly is not uncommon.

Fortunately, the reverse can happen. A funeral director called on a Thursday and asked if I could conduct a funeral on the following Monday. After finding out more about the situation, I agreed. The deceased was a man in his late eighties who had lived much of his life in the city, but finished his life in a retirement home in another city where two of his children lived. One was his daughter, and the other was one of two sons. The other son lived in a suburb of the home city, where the funeral was to happen. The body was being flown in from the other city, and the only time all the family members, including a few additional relatives, would be together was at the funeral.

I arrived at the funeral home a half hour before the funeral was to begin in order to meet the family members, so that at least we would not be total strangers. After we had sat and talked for a few minutes, someone remarked that one of the brothers had not arrived at the funeral home yet. This caused some anxiety, because time was growing short until the funeral was scheduled to begin. This is when the daughter informed me about her brother, the alcoholic. He lived in her city and had come with her to attend the funeral at her urging, though she had little contact with him normally. He had missed the funeral of their mother, and she and her other brother were determined that he was not going to miss this one. They had checked him into a hotel a short cab ride away from the funeral home, yet he was nowhere in sight as time for the funeral approached.

A cousin volunteered to retrieve him from the hotel, if we were willing to wait. I agreed. We waited for thirty minutes, which is the only time I have ever experienced a funeral starting late. When I saw the cousin and the brother walk into the funeral home at last, I must confess that I was surprised at how much he looked the part of an alcoholic brother, the black sheep of the family. He looked twice his age and wore an ill-fitting suit he probably would not wear again for years.

The funeral was brief, and only a handful of relatives were present, but it seemed meaningful. Perhaps there are those who would say that we should not have waited and that the brother should have missed the funeral. For my part, it required a snap decision in a unique situation. Looking back, I am glad I waited because I believe the family did care for the brother. And I know that funerals leave lifelong memories. I knew nothing about the relationship between the alcoholic brother and his deceased father. Perhaps he would have preferred not to attend the funeral. Yet he did board a plane, and he did shed a tear at the funeral. Who knows what difference this may make in family relations at some future point and in his personal life. After all, he did have the experience of seeing that he could tolerate this emotional experience and survive it, even though it must have been very difficult for him.

Families in Conflict

Here is a whole book in itself. It would be easy to collect dozens of funeral stories about families that fight during funerals. Family members will stop you as you enter the funeral home for the visitation in order to tell you about their evil brother, sister, aunt, uncle, or cousin. They will have arguments five minutes before the funeral is to start. They will cause a scene at the meal following the funeral, depending on who sits where. Sometimes the funeral is an occasion for bringing a long-standing family feud out into the open. In other instances, dysfunctional family systems generate conflict as grieving family members handle their interactions poorly.

A sixteen-year-old named Jimmy grew up in a very chaotic and violent family. Finally, he ran away from home because both his parents were alcoholics, and his father beat him one too many times. He stayed with friends and continued attending school. He even initiated conversations with a school counselor who identified him as a "troubled youth who had potential." Something must have clicked between them, because the counselor and her husband became foster parents and brought Jimmy to live with them.

Jimmy had been living with his foster parents almost a year when he died in a car wreck. He ran his foster parents' car off the road, hit a tree, and was killed instantly. One other boy was in the car and was hurt but not killed.

The foster parents' minister learned that there was extensive blame flying back and forth between Jimmy's foster and biological parents. In addition, they fought over who would handle the funeral arrangements, though the biological parents had not had much to do with Jimmy since he ran away. They not only fought over where the funeral would be and who would officiate, but over where he would be buried. Finally, they reached a compromise. The visitation would be at a funeral home in

Jimmy's old neighborhood. Then there would be a graveside service at the cemetery in the foster parents' community, with their minister officiating. The foster family would pay the expenses.

At the graveside service, the minister stood at the head of the casket. To her left, on one side of the casket, were the foster family, some church members, and some teachers and students from school. To her right, on the other side of the casket, was Jimmy's birth family. The minister could tell that Jimmy's biological parents had been drinking, along with one of Jimmy's three brothers. Another brother had to be released from jail to attend the service, and he came in the company of an armed marshal. The two sets of people glared at each other so intensely during the service that the minister hoped no one would fly across the casket and start a fight. The sermon was about the reconciling love of God, and in the sermon she noted the one thing the two families had in common was love for Jimmy. Afterward she remarked, "We got through it."

Family conflict at funerals is not always that dramatic. A man in his nineties died, leaving behind two middle-aged sons and a wife, who was their stepmother. The deceased man had stipulated in papers for his final arrangements that he would be cremated and that his ashes were to be buried in an urn.

An argument arose when the two sons came to the memorial service at the church, of which neither was a member any longer. A mere ten minutes before the service, they started arguing over whether the urn should be on the baptismal font or on the communion table. The minister said it could not be either place, but that it could be placed on a stand. Then the underlying issue emerged. The married son wanted his father's ashes, but the other son wanted to follow his father's instructions. In addition, he did not want to upset his stepmother, who was over ninety herself, by changing the plans. She had cared for her husband during the past two decades, while he suffered from strokes.

The minister suggested perhaps there was a third way, rather than the ashes going one place or the other. Almost immediately, the brother who wanted the ashes found the third way, saying, "Well, if I could just have some of Dad's ashes, it would be OK." The other brother agreed that this would be acceptable if they could be removed by the funeral director and placed in a smaller urn behind closed doors, so that their stepmother would not have to be upset. They talked to the funeral director, who said not to worry; he would take care of it. They had the memorial service with no further difficulties.

Couples

Sometimes a couple makes funeral arrangements together, and the minister ends up having pre-funeral conversations with them. Even though the couple may have children, as well as other relatives, the minister will not necessarily see them, depending on circumstances.

In one such conversation, the minister had scheduled a time to meet with a woman and her husband. They had to drive across a large city, so they combined several tasks in their trip, one of which was stopping by the church to talk to the minister about the funeral. The deceased was the woman's mother, who died at age eighty-six. Both she and her daughter had maintained their membership in the congregation, though they had not attended in years because they lived so far away. The minister originally found out about the death by returning a call to a funeral director who had left a message at his office. After hanging up, he called the daughter. The husband answered and told the minister his wife was at work arranging her schedule, getting time off for the funeral. The husband seemed to want to talk, so the minister had what amounted to a pastoral care conversation with the husband over the phone. He was grieving the loss of his mother-in-law, and he talked about his relationship with her and about his role in the family during her final few years of declining health.

That evening, the minister called again, and this time the daughter answered. She declined the minister's offer to visit, but a meeting in the minister's office was scheduled for the next day during the trip into the city. In the meeting, she proved to be far more anxious and resistant to talking about her mother than the husband. The minister also observed that she tried to keep her husband from saying much about the deceased by cutting off his conversation. In her anxiety, she was trying to control not only herself, but those around her. The children were in school and did not attend the meeting.

The daughter's anxious and controlling behavior made a strong impression on the minister and affected his funeral preparation later that day. On the one hand, he pondered whether he should give in to the daughter's control by planning a generic funeral. He could do this, for example, by not mentioning the name of the deceased in any of the prayers and by avoiding family stories in the sermon. By generalizing rather than being specific, he could help the mourners control their emotions. On the other hand, he pondered whether he should resist the daughter's control and plan a more personal funeral by naming names, including family stories he had learned from the husband, and including a story from his own experience of the deceased woman from a few years back. He decided this was the healthier course of action. However, he feared the daughter would be displeased with the funeral, or even become angry with him. The thing that helped him fight his fear and stick with his choice was the recognition that the funeral was for all the mourners, including the husband, children, other relatives, church members who were longtime friends of the deceased, and strangers who would be attending.

Conclusion

Caring for bereaved individuals and families has many facets. In pastoral ministry, pre-funeral care and planning is expected with those who arrange funerals, but there is care beyond what is expected. Sometimes care involves having huge doses of patience. Meaningful things can happen, as in the burial of Margaret's ashes. Sometimes it involves making snap judgments, even though the outcome is uncertain. Sometimes it involves helping resolve a conflict, even at the funeral or memorial service itself. Often this means practical problem solving. Finally, non–family members grieve and mourn, and they will be discussed in the next chapter.

CHAPTER FIVE

Caring for Mourners Beyond
the Family

Grief often cannot be confined to family members. Others who grieve may be individuals, including children, teens, and adults of all ages. They may be a couple or a family in the church who has been good friends with another couple or family in the church, but who suddenly find themselves dealing with a widow, a widower, grieving parents, or grieving children. They may be a group within the church that has been together for many years, but who now has lost a beloved group member. Or they may be the congregation as a whole, and if the congregation as a whole grieves, you can bet that many in the local community grieve, too. If there is to be pastoral care for those beyond the family who grieve, it typically comes by means of the funeral.

Keep in mind that we are considering just the time from the point of death through the funeral. Also, though the minister cannot talk to many mourners before the funeral, there is mutual care among church members, some of whom may have the opportunity to talk before the funeral. Expressions of care among church members often are seen at the visitation before the funeral or memorial service. Sometimes this even extends to family members caring for others. Though the main emphasis is on the family, there may be times when supportive, comforting expressions of care may be mutual between family members and a friend or acquaintance who grieves the loss along with the family.

In this chapter, bereavement situations emphasizing mourners beyond the family will be discussed. Although grieving families will not be omitted, they will be placed in the larger context of others grieving and mourning in the church and community.

Mourners Who Belong to a Group within the Congregation

In the psychological understanding of grief, it is common to cite the circumstances of the death as a factor contributing to the individual's grief response, as we saw in chapter 3. When considering those who grieve in the church and community beyond the family members, the circumstances of a death continue playing an important role. In one kind of circumstance, the church member who dies has participated in a particular group within the congregation, such as a Sunday school class, for enough time that emotional connections have developed, friendships have grown, and the person has become part of the group. Others in the congregation may know this person, but not as well as the group members, because the group members spend time together on a regular basis and get to know each other beyond what is possible for the congregation as a whole.

Ministers and church members get to know the various groups in the congregation. They get to know who participates in the groups and who is a friend of whom. When a group member dies, the minister and others in the church think of the group in terms of its loss and think of close friends who may have been together for years in the church. This in no way opposes thinking of the family first and foremost. Rather, it is in addition to a focus on the family members, who themselves may think about the group and close personal friends in the church. This, of course, assumes there is a family, which is not always the case. Or, there are adult children who have not been in the community for many years, in which case the minister and church members may be aware of needing to care for the family members as they arrive in the community, while also being aware of grieving church members, about whom the adult children may know little or nothing.

A minister, Rev. Carson, found herself in a situation like this when a choir member in her congregation, Nancy Roberts, died. Years ago, Nancy had raised her two young daughters as a single parent after her husband died of cancer and left her with staggering medical bills. She struggled for years to support her family and pay the bills. Over time, she became a jazz singer in the city and was well respected both as a musician and as a voice and piano teacher, though she still had to do secretarial work in order to support herself financially. At sixty, she too died of cancer after suffering from it for three years. Nancy had never remarried, and the only family she had left included her two daughters, one son-in-law, and one grandchild. The older daughter, Mary, lived in a distant city with her husband and child, and the younger daughter, Alice, lived in another distant city. She was single. Both daughters were in their thirties when their mother died.

Rev. Carson had been at the church for two years when Nancy became a member. This was a five-hundred-member Protestant church in an urban neighborhood. Like so many, Nancy became a church member through her association with one of the members, who happened to be her employer. Tim Jackson owned a music business, and Nancy was his bookkeeper. Soon after beginning her job, she was diagnosed with cancer and had a mastectomy. It was after this that she joined the church, attending a Sunday school class and singing in the choir. This is when she asked permission to give music lessons at the church, in the room where the choir practiced, in order to earn a living.

About the time of her second mastectomy, she moved into a little apartment across the street from the church, in a building owned by church members. She continued teaching as she could and began helping out in the church office. As the cancer progressed, church members increasingly assumed responsibility for her care. For example, some brought food when she was too sick to cook, and they did grocery shopping for her. Others drove her to the doctor's office for appointments and cancer treatments. These were choir members at first. But eventually they asked for help from the congregation's care team. At least ten people ended up caring for Nancy on a regular basis. During this time, the minister visited her at home and during her periodic stays in the hospital. Before the second mastectomy, they had talked at church, because she was working there several days a week.

Nancy prided herself on not being sentimental. When she began to talk about dying, she said she didn't want to have any kind of funeral service and that she was donating her body to the local medical school. She had not told her daughters the truth about her illness, that she was dying. At long last, however, some choir members prevailed on her to tell her daughters the true situation. This occurred around the time when she was becoming too ill to work at all. In response to this news, both daughters visited her, coordinating their visits so that one daughter stayed for a week, followed by the second daughter during the second week. Each had to return to work after taking a week off.

At the same time, Rev. Carson observed that choir members and care team members were continuing to care for Nancy with energy and love, and now their practical help was daily. Also, a feeling of deep concern for Nancy had developed in the congregation as a whole. As she thought about what it was going to be like for "members grieving, yet having nowhere to take that grief if they didn't have some kind of service," she realized that there needed to be a memorial service when the time came.

So during her next visit, Rev. Carson asked Nancy if they could have a simple memorial service at the church. Nancy responded, "I don't want a service where people are going to say things about me that are going to make me sound nicer than I am."

"Nancy, the service is not for you. We are all going to have deep feelings that we need to share. The service is for us," Rev. Carson said.

"I'll think about it," Nancy said.

A week later, Nancy gave Rev. Carson permission to have a memorial service at the church. At this point, Nancy was in "pretty bad shape," and Rev. Carson was not able to talk to her about why she changed her mind. She had been straightforward with Nancy when she asked permission to have a memorial service, but she had not pressured her, which would have been inappropriate.

During this same visit, while Rev. Carson was in the bedroom with Nancy, one of Nancy's daughters, Mary, was in another part of the apartment. It had been three weeks since her first visit, and now she was back. Before she left, Rev. Carson spoke to Mary but did not tell her that Nancy had given permission for a memorial service. Somehow, it did not "feel right" to mention it at that time.

Early the next morning, Nancy was admitted to the hospital. It became evident that she would not be returning home, so Mary called her sister, Alice, informing her of the situation. Nancy died around 4 a.m. on the second day of her hospitalization, with Mary present. She called Rev. Carson, who drove to the hospital and sat with Mary as she sobbed for a long time. Then she helped Mary deal with practicalities, including signing papers and gathering Nancy's things. Church members were called later in the morning by the care team of the church.

Later that same morning, Alice arrived by plane, and Rev. Carson met with Mary and Alice at 11:00 a.m. at Nancy's apartment. She told them Nancy had given her permission to have a memorial service at the church, and then she asked for their permission. They were surprised, but they thought about it and agreed that it was all right to have a memorial service. Then she offered them the opportunity to talk about the service, but they did not want to make any decisions about its content. They said that this was her church, so let the church take care of that. Mary's husband and child came for the service.

Nancy died on a Thursday, and the memorial service was scheduled for the following Sunday afternoon at three. This meant that Rev. Carson would have to finish preparing for Sunday morning, and she also would have to prepare for Sunday afternoon. She thought that because Nancy's daughters had no requests for the service, she would be planning it alone. Instead, she started getting phone calls from choir members and a few others with suggestions for the memorial service. For instance, the choir director had "firm ideas" about which hymns to sing. Also, a choir member wanted to sing a solo, which he had sung as a duet with Nancy at a very meaningful church gathering two years earlier. Still other choir members suggested scripture passages to read in the service. From outside the congregation, one of Nancy's voice students requested that they play a recording of "Adagio for Strings" by Samuel Barber, which he said was one of Nancy's favorites. She had introduced him to that music, and they had listened to it together. He volunteered to bring the recording and play it himself. Finally, the women's organization in the church volunteered to organize a reception in the church's fellowship hall following the service.

At the memorial service were Nancy's two daughters, Mary's husband and child, choir members, care team members, other church members, musicians in the city's jazz community, and many of her music students. One student, an Orthodox Jewish cantor, stood through the entire service outside the sanctuary in the narthex, because he was not allowed by his faith to enter the sanctuary.

The memorial service was forty minutes long, with the music, the scripture readings, prayers, and the sermon. No one spoke about Nancy except Rev. Carson in the sermon, so that Nancy's request to have no tributes would be honored. After the service, no one left. First, they stood in the sanctuary and talked. Then they went downstairs for the reception and talked some more. Rev. Carson summed up the experience by saying that there was a "feeling among the church members that they had done the right thing for her."

A choir member died, and the group in the church most affected was the choir, along with some care team members. Although others in the congregation grieved too, the congregation as a whole seemed to be in the background, supporting those who had been on the front lines, engaging in hands-on care over several years.

Congregational Trauma and Grief: The Loss of a Minister

Another congregational circumstance involves a death that has the effect of traumatizing the entire congregation. In this circumstance, the congregation as a whole grieves and mourns those who die tragically and suddenly. Jill Hudson brings this point home in her book, *Congregational Trauma: Caring, Coping and Learning,* when she writes:

> Murder. Arson. Bombings. Airline crashes. Pedophilia. Suicide. Newspaper exposes. Lover's revenge. Do these sound like the topics of a *New York Times* best-seller list? Yes, but they are also real-life happenings that touched the church of Jesus Christ over the past three years. I refer not to individuals in particular congregations who were affected by such atrocious acts, but to entire communities of faith that were directly struck by events we would label traumatic. (1998, vii)

Since she wrote those words, the terrorism of September 11, 2001, which destroyed the twin towers of the World Trade Center in New York City, has given "airline crashes" and "suicide" a whole new meaning for contemporary societies throughout the world. This large, societal situation helps us see more easily how death can bring trauma to groups of different sizes and that sometimes these groups can be communities of faith. Hudson defines the trauma of congregations as "the large-scale effect of a sudden, unexpected crisis event on a large group of people— namely the system we call a *congregation.* Trauma is initially overwhelming. It permanently changes the environment and the lives of all who exist within it" (1998, 16).

Hudson experienced such a congregational trauma in her ministry as the executive presbyter of a presbytery in the Presbyterian Church (USA). A church in her presbytery lost both its minister and the minister's spouse through a brutal double murder in their home late one night just before Christmas. Not only were they murdered; their house was burned to the ground. It was after midnight when the phone awakened Rev. Hudson, as the associate minister was calling to inform her of the deaths. By 3 a.m., she and the staff, having been to the crime scene, gathered at the church and were joined by the police chaplain, who called an adult child of the deceased at his home in another city, after the state police arrived there: "I have some information for you which will be difficult to hear. Last evening sometime between 9:00 and 11:00, your parents were bound and murdered with an ax in their home" (32). One of the circumstances making a traumatic event more difficult is that all the information may not be available immediately, but may be learned in bits and pieces, as Hudson explains: "This was the first we had heard of the actual details of their death. A wave of disbelief washed over our small gathering. How could this be? Who would have done such an unfathomable act?" (32). Soon these questions echoed through the congregation and community.

Hudson also discusses the case of a church in another denomination in which the congregation became traumatized on learning that their minister committed suicide. After becoming worn down from a seemingly intractable conflict within the congregation, the minister set fire to the church building. He became a suspect in the ensuing investigation, and he finally shot himself to death after leaving two notes, one confessing that he had set the fire and the other written to his family and the church (40–44). Finally, Hudson discusses the case of the Oklahoma City bombing of 1995, telling the stories of some ministers who helped care for the traumatized community (44–53).

There are several substantial differences between the bereavement situation involving an individual, a family, or a group within the congregation, and one involving a traumatized congregation, from the time of the death through the funeral and beyond. One difference is that outside help may be needed at the time of the death. When it is the minister of the church who dies, someone else must assist in caring for the family and congregation. If, for instance, a traumatized congregation has lost its senior minister, but has one or more associate ministers, they certainly lead in caring for the congregation, but they too are likely to be traumatized, along with lay leaders. The same may be true if it is the associate minister who dies. Others from the church governing body must step in and assist, working in conjunction with ministers and lay leaders (1998, 119–22).

Another difference involves the local community. If the situation is significant enough to traumatize the entire congregation, it undoubtedly affects the community. The police may be investigating the death, and the local press may cover the story, which means that church leaders must deal with the press and police (1998, 102–18).

A third difference is the extent of funeral planning that must take place. The funeral planning typically going on within the bereaved family, such as talking to the funeral director and minister, now encompasses the congregation and community. For instance, where the funeral is to be held now becomes a major concern. Rather than considering only the usual two choices, the funeral home or the church sanctuary, the family now may choose to have the funeral in a large auditorium, because more space will be needed to contain the worshipers.

Finally, the death of the minister raises the question of the relationship between the minister and the congregation as a whole, as well as the question of the relationship between the minister and church members within the congregation. As the psychological understanding of grief teaches, those who grieve have an emotional attachment to the deceased. A congregation is invested emotionally in its minister. Any church member, or any group within the church, or any church representative speaking for the congregation as a whole who says that the deceased was "our minister" is conveying that there was an emotional dimension to the relationship. Although there are other important features of this relationship, the emotional dimension is enough to involve all the church members in grief when the minister dies. At the same time, as Hudson indicates, not everyone in the congregation will have the same response to the death because there is significant individuality in grief:

> It is important to point out that trauma and grief are suffered both by the individuals who make up the congregation and by the church as a whole. Because grief is unique to each person, the point where an entire congregation finds itself in the process is not easily assessed. It is easy to confuse where the congregation

may be with where a few highly visible or articulate individuals seem to be. (28)

It is very understandable that a congregation would be traumatized upon the death of its minister, especially when the death is sudden, unexpected and gruesome. In this case, it seems to be a matter of course that many people in addition to family members grieve the loss. But there are other deaths, too, that can result in congregational trauma and grief.

Congregational Trauma and Grief: The Loss of Church Members

A third circumstance also involves congregational trauma, except the death is that of one or more church members rather than the minister. The congregation as a whole grieves and mourns the loss, but extensive assistance from church leaders outside the congregation is not needed, as when the minister dies.

Let's follow the experience of a minister named John Scott during what I called funeral time in chapter 1. He is married to Angie, and they have three small children. This man, in his early thirties, is pastoring his second church and has been there for five years. The congregation is an old, established Protestant church of approximately 160 members located in a small town not far from a large city. Like many such places, it has members who have lived in the community for their entire lives, mixed with those who moved there because of business. The town could be characterized as a "college town" because a large state university is located there.

As an experienced minister, Rev. Scott had officiated at funerals over the years, but now he was faced with a bereavement situation beyond his previous experience. One weekday morning, while driving to school on a lonely stretch of road, two teenage sisters, who were members of Rev. Scott's congregation, died in a one-car accident. There were no witnesses, so little is known about the accident except that somehow the car got out of control, flipped over, and hit a tree, most likely killing the young women instantly.

The two sisters who died were Carol, age sixteen, and Ann, age thirteen. There were no other brothers or sisters in the family. Their parents, George and Julie Jacobs, were natives of the community. George had grown up in the congregation and was a third-generation church member, whereas Julie had joined when they married. They had raised their daughters in the congregation. Rev. Scott had known George's parents, who were members, and he had known Julie's father. Since coming to the church, he had officiated at the funerals of all three parents. Julie's mother was still living.

Now, the parents, other family members, personal friends of Carol and Ann, friends of the parents, the congregation as a whole, and the community itself were traumatized over these two sudden, tragic deaths. To make matters worse, there had been a rash of teenage deaths in the community over the past five years due to automobile accidents, so that one response to the current deaths was "not again!"

Thursday

On a Thursday morning at 9:00 a.m., Rev. Scott was about to get into his car and drive to the nearby city for an appointment when his wife called out to him that he needed to phone the local high school. The church secretary had called to give him that message. He called the school, but getting no answer, he called the church office and talked to the church secretary, who said, "Go to the high school. George and Julie have lost both their girls." He and his wife arrived at the school around fifteen minutes later and were met by the police chief, who told them that Carol and Ann had died in a one-car accident.

The parents, George and Julie, along with George's uncle Mark, were in a room waiting for Rev. Scott. After talking to the police chief, he and Angie went to them and stayed with them most of the morning. There were hugs and tears and consoling words. The parents seemed "broken apart."

Gradually, Rev. Scott learned more of the story. Julie often drove her daughter Ann to school because she worked in the school system, but she was running late that morning. And because the middle school that Ann attended was right next to Carol's high school, it was convenient for Ann to ride with Carol. However, Carol was running late that morning also, and she was to pick up a friend on the way to school. So it was thought that perhaps Carol was speeding and lost control of the car on a hilly county road with narrow shoulders.

George had been the first parent to discover the deaths. When he was driving to work on the same road, he came upon the scene of the wreck, where police cars were directing traffic. The worst proved to be true, and in his devastation the police drove him to the high school to be with Julie, who had arrived there for work.

As the morning wore on, Julie was visited by many of her colleagues, who came by the room to express their condolences. Several teachers had taught one or both of the girls, and providing support and comfort was mixed with their own grief.

During this time Rev. Scott "did many things." First, he made a list of people who should be contacted about the deaths. Then he had to make a decision about activities going on at the church that evening. After consideration, he canceled a meeting and choir practice, deciding instead to hold a prayer service at 7:00 p.m. This was communicated to church members through the congregation's prayer chain, but word quickly got around town and to the schools. Finally, he agreed to accompany George's cousin Mark to inform Julie's mother, Ann and Carol's grandmother, about the deaths.

The family made plans to return to their house and left shortly before noon. Angie accompanied them in their car, while Rev. Scott drove his car first to the church office, where he received a call from the mayor offering to help in any way he could. Then he met the cousin at the grandmother's nursing home, where they told her about the deaths. She suffered from Alzheimer's disease, which prevented her from fully grasping the news. Rev. Scott noted that she did not "break down," but that she did make comments, such as "Carol is a good driver," and that she did ask questions repeatedly, such as "Where did it happen?"

Cousin Mark took the grandmother to the parents' house, and Rev. Scott drove there in his car and stayed until 3:30 p.m. Soon after he arrived, he sat with the family as they heard the sheriff's report on the accident. There were the facts of the accident, as far as they were known. There was the preliminary report from the coroner's office confirming that the sisters died instantly. There were details relevant to insurance and discussion about reports and how to receive them. After this, Rev. Scott helped out by phoning some relatives who lived out of state, informing them of the deaths, and he had a preliminary planning conversation with the funeral director over the phone. Otherwise, he provided a "general presence" to the stream of people who dropped by and to family members arriving who lived within driving distance. Then he went home to plan the prayer service.

Rev. Scott arrived at church at 6:30 p.m., at which time he had an interview with a television reporter from the nearby city, who had called him while he was preparing the service. He was asked such questions as "What were the girls like?" and "What do you say to a family in this time?" He had determined beforehand that he wanted to convey a healthy view of the community grieving, and he felt that he was able to do this by saying in the interview that the community was coming together in response to the deaths. He also was determined to avoid clichés, such as "it was God's will." He indicated clearly that the deaths were accidental, a point he reiterated in the funeral sermon a few days later.

After helping church members set up extra chairs in the sanctuary, he began the prayer service. Around 250 people attended the forty-five minute service, including church members, many teenagers and their parents, and others from the community, but the bereaved family did not attend. The service began with a passage from Psalm 46, which reads: "God is our refuge and strength, a very present help in trouble." A prayer followed the reading. It began: "Almighty God, our creator and redeemer, you are our comfort and strength. You have given us our sisters Carol and Ann to know and to love in our pilgrimage on earth."

The rest of the service included several series of liturgical elements. Each series began with a hymn, followed by a scripture reading, a prayer, and two minutes of silence. For the prayers, Rev. Scott drew on denominational resources, other books, and the Internet. Following the service, many stayed and talked for an hour.

Friday

In the morning, Rev. Scott completed the Sunday bulletin, despite the number of phone calls dealing with funeral plans and with more offers of assistance than there were opportunities to help. According to Rev. Scott,

> When things like this happen, a pastor has an incredible amount of discretion to ask people to do things, and they'll do them. But, in the days after the accident, there was more desire to do something than there were things to do. Everybody wanted to do something to help, but nobody could do the only thing that would have helped, which was to bring the girls back. So, we busied ourselves with a lot of other things around the events of the funeral, the visitation and getting ready for all of that. It wasn't just the congregation, it was the community.

At 3:00 p.m., Rev. Scott met George and Julie, along with cousin Mark and his wife, Anita, at the funeral home to make plans with the funeral director. It is relatively rare for the minister to go with the family to the funeral home, but in this instance of congregational and community trauma, it made good sense because of the need for communication among a variety of people in relation to planning. The funeral home meeting lasted five hours, which also is highly unusual, but it took this much time to get done what needed to be done.

Some parts of the meeting included what typically may take place between the bereaved family and the funeral director, including such things as putting the obituary together, determining where memorials should be sent, choosing the casket, deciding the day and time of the funeral, deciding whether there would be music so that a musician could be contacted, and naming who would officiate at the funeral, which of course was Rev. Scott. In addition, a decision about where to have the visitation and funeral had to be made, which was where Rev. Scott's presence at the meeting became especially helpful.

It was decided that the visitation would be at the church but that the funeral would be at the auditorium of the local university, so that a large number of people could attend. Because of the large numbers, there were logistical problems to figure out, requiring cooperation and good communication between the minister, the funeral director, high school officials, the sheriff, the local police, state troopers, and officials from the university. Once permission to have the funeral at the auditorium was secured from the university, traffic and parking problems had to be resolved, which required help from the police, sheriff, and troopers. Also, the high school officials allowed buses to be used so that people could be driven to the auditorium for the funeral. This helped resolve the parking problem. When Rev. Scott finally got home after the meeting, he made a phone call arranging to meet a university official at the auditorium the next morning.

Saturday

Rev. Scott looked the auditorium over in order to get a feel for what the funeral would be like in such a huge place, and he needed to see if there were any practical problems to be addressed.

That afternoon, when he sat down to finish writing the sermon for Sunday, he found it very difficult to focus on anything but the accident. After wrestling with this for a while, he called his counselor for support, which proved to be helpful. Afterward, he was able to concentrate on the sermon and finish it.

Sunday

Then came Sunday morning worship. Sometimes, when there has been a death in the congregation, the Sunday worship will occur before the funeral or memorial service. It can be an awkward situation, especially when large numbers of church members are affected. On the one hand, there is a need to address the death, but on the other hand, the worship service is not a de facto funeral service. This is not an all or nothing situation, however. There are a variety of ways to address the death or deaths appropriately in the worship service.

Rev. Scott handled the situation by announcing that the sisters had died, giving a brief overview of what had happened on the remote chance that there was someone who did not yet know about the deaths. He also communicated the funeral plans to the congregation, and included the bereaved in his pastoral prayer. Finally, he alluded to the situation in his sermon, but overall he stayed with his original sermon topic. Julie and George did not attend the worship service, but Mark and Anita were there.

On Sunday afternoon at 3:00 p.m., Rev. Scott was scheduled to meet with the bereaved family at their home. This was to be the traditional time of discussing the funeral, giving family members the opportunity to make any requests, such as including certain scripture, music, or speakers in the service, and it was to be a time of remembering their deceased daughters. When he arrived, Rev. Scott found that the Jacobs had invited their daughters' closest friends to participate. There were seven or eight teenage girls present, along with a few of their mothers. Several others also participated in the discussion, including Mark and Anita and a few friends of Julie. The conversation took place as people continually dropped by the house.

Special music was chosen, and there were requests that a letter being written by George's sister be read, along with some poems being written by friends of the two dead sisters.

Next, Rev. Scott asked each of the participants to think of a word to describe Ann and a word to describe Carol. This proved to be fruitful, and Julie "set the tone." The word she thought of for both daughters was *miracle,* which led to her telling the group about the birth of each. When Carol was born, she had some physical difficulties and her survival was uncertain for a time. But she lived, and this was the first miracle. Then when Ann was born, Julie had a difficult time and came close to death. But she lived, and this was the second miracle. Her point was that she had tremendous gratitude for the time she had with her daughters. Rev. Scott experienced Julie's story as a sign of her faith, in the sense that expressing gratitude and thanks for her daughters contrasted with the many expressions of how horrible the accident had been, often voiced since the deaths.

As the teenagers and other adults continued the discussion, sharing their words and stories, Rev. Scott began to get a feel for the personalities of Ann and Carol as seen through the eyes of family and friends, and he was able to reflect some of what he learned in the funeral sermon. This is not an extraneous part of remembering the deceased through storytelling. Although it is important for those present to tell and listen to the stories about the deceased, it also may contribute to the funeral, becoming helpful to every mourner, if the minister can appropriately and sensitively reflect in the funeral what is learned from the storytelling.

According to Rev. Scott, there was "excellent sharing, which many commented on long after." The teenage friends of Carol and Ann found the group discussion meaningful and proudly told others that they helped plan the funeral. Perhaps because this bereavement situation included a traumatized congregation and community, those who participated in the funeral discussion at the home of the family represented the many who grieved, all of whom needed to hear about the conversation and share in it indirectly.

When an entire congregation and community is traumatized, there are what Rev. Scott called "layers" of grief. He identified some of these layers, beginning with those individuals most affected because they were closest to the deceased sisters. As you would expect, the deepest layer included the parents, along with other family members. Another layer included the best friends of Ann and Carol, followed by other teenage friends who were not quite as close as the best friends. Then there were adults and their children, who were family friends. There were teachers who knew the sisters and teachers who had children who knew the sisters.

All these individuals and families were part of the traumatized community, which comprised the most encompassing layer of grief. The editor of the local newspaper symbolized the community grief when he remarked, "What a lousy day to run a newspaper."

The traumatized congregation formed its own layer of grief, within the larger layer of the community. Recall from the first case presented in this chapter that a group within the congregation grieved the loss of a beloved member. In Rev. Scott's church, something similar seemed to be happening, only on a larger scale. Rather than the grief being associated primarily with a group within the church, the congregation as a whole grieved the losses. It was a small congregation in which the Jacobs family was well known. They were active in the church, participating in various ways. George was a deacon, and Julie had been on the committee that called Rev. Scott. In the Christmas Eve service, less than a month before the deaths, the family had lit the Christ candle.

On Sunday night, Rev. Scott put together the funeral service so that the bulletin could go to the printer on Monday. Depending on tradition and circumstance, there may or may not be a bulletin at the funeral. In this instance, it was wise to have one, because there would be a huge number of participants from the community, many of whom would not know the religious tradition.

Monday

Are you tired yet? I'm exhausted. Just imagine what it must have been like for Rev. Scott, not to mention the family and others closest to the situation. At 9:00 a.m., he met with the funeral director, the police, the sheriff, and security from the university to work out final details for the service. Then he returned to the church to oversee setup for the visitation, held at the church.

George and Julie, along with other family members, arrived at the church at noon. After Rev. Scott said a prayer with them, Julie and George viewed the bodies alone, followed by the rest of the family. The visitation began at 2:00 p.m. and was scheduled to end at 8:00 p.m., but it lasted until 10:00 p.m., as nearly 1,300 people visited.

The caskets were placed in a room called the parlor, while a long line filed by, including many teenagers. The line snaked through the sanctuary, which is where the teens congregated after going through the line. This was quite an emotional scene, which led to Rev. Scott's observation that "grief spreads like wildfire." He finally went home at 11:00 p.m.

Tuesday

At 4:30 a.m., Rev. Scott awoke to begin writing his funeral sermon. Given what he had been through, you can see how this unusual time for writing became necessary. By 9:00 a.m., he had printed out the sermon, showered and dressed, and picked up the bulletins and delivered them to the university auditorium, where the funeral was to be held at 1:00 p.m.

The auditorium was large and relatively impersonal, which Rev. Scott tried to counteract by bringing furniture from the church sanctuary, including the communion table, a cross, the baptismal font, candles, a flower stand, two chairs, paraments, and banners. This turned out to be especially helpful to some church members, because they had begun to feel lost in the crowd. They had not had nearly as much personal contact with the grieving parents as they would have had under more typical circumstances, but this changed after the funeral.

Here is the order of worship as printed in the bulletin:

Sentences of Scripture
Hymn (all hymns and the Gloria Patri were printed as inserts in the
    bulletin)
Prayer
Call to Confession
Prayer of Confession (printed in the bulletin, read in unison)
Silent Prayers of Confession
Declaration of Forgiveness
Gloria Patri
Old Testament Scripture Readings
Hymn
New Testament Scripture Readings

The letter and poems were interspersed with scripture readings. Rev. Scott read the letter written by George's sister and a poem written by a female friend of Ann. The minister who preceded Scott at the church read a poem written by a male friend of Carol.

Sermon (preached by Rev. Scott, ten to fifteen minutes long)
Special Music (a duet by choir members of the congregation)
Affirmation of Faith, the Apostles' Creed (printed in the bulletin)
Prayers of Thanksgiving, Supplication, and Intercession
The Lord's Prayer (printed in the bulletin)
Hymn
Commendation (a responsive reading printed in the bulletin)
Blessing (benediction)

The funeral service ended at 2:00 p.m., and forty-five minutes later the procession to the cemetery began. Many mourners gathered at the gravesite for the committal, which included the following:

Scripture Sentences
Words of Committal

Prayers
Blessing

The time at the cemetery ended at 3:45 p.m., which meant that there was only one thing left for the family to do. The fifty family members gathered at the church for a meal prepared and hosted by church members. It was a fitting ending to a day that had just become an important part of this family's history, the congregation's history, and the community's history.

Conclusion

Many may grieve in addition to family members when there is a death in the church. Individuals, couples, families, and groups within the congregation, as well as the congregation and community, may grieve the death of one or more beloved church members or ministers. The circumstances surrounding such deaths can be as variable as the groups of mourners who are influenced by those circumstances. Pastoral ministry in these times must be flexible, so that ministers can respond effectively to the realities of the situation. It goes without saying that ministers must respond with an attitude of loving care for the bereaved, but this includes more than personal contact. This contact is mixed with public leadership in preparation for the funeral or memorial service and culminates in worship leadership in these services, including the committal. It often ends with the fellowship of a meal.

It is evident that funerals are important to the bereaved. In the next chapter, funerals will be explored directly.

CHAPTER SIX

Assembling for a Funeral

If you are to conduct a funeral, preparing it is half the battle. But what is a funeral? Preparing a funeral presupposes that you have some understanding of it. In this chapter, the funeral will be discussed, including the definition of a funeral, an understanding of the specifically Christian funeral, and instructions for conducting a Christian funeral based on liturgical books in several denominations.

Christians did not invent funerals. They existed long before Christianity and continue to be part of human societies and religions throughout the world. So let's look first at an understanding of funerals that includes Christianity but goes beyond it, and then at Christian funerals specifically, in preparation for exploring funeral liturgies in the second half of this chapter and in the next.

Defining the Funeral

When the *Oxford English Dictionary* defines a funeral as "the ceremonies connected with the burial (or cremation, etc.) of the body of a dead person," this definition must be understood more broadly than as just referring to one religious tradition. This broadness is seen in the word *ceremony*, which the same dictionary defines as "an outward rite or observance." A ceremony may be "religious or held sacred." Or it may not have an explicit connection to religion, being simply "a formal act or series of acts prescribed by ritual, protocol, or convention" (*Merriam-Webster's Collegiate Dictionary*). Whether or not *ceremony* is seen as inherently religious, it applies to non-Christian and to Christian funerals.

It is especially appropriate that the word *ceremony* is used for defining a funeral, because of its history. *Cere* has the ancient root meaning of "wax." A cerecloth is a cloth smeared with wax, making it waterproof, formerly used for wrapping a dead body. In related definitions, *cere* can mean "to anoint with spices," "to embalm," and "to shut up (a corpse in a coffin)."

A funeral ceremony, seen as an "outward rite" or "formal act," involves putting into practice, or performing, what a funeral ritual prescribes. Notice that the word *rite* is used to define *ceremony*, but it also is used interchangeably with *ceremony*, so that a funeral ceremony is the same thing as a funeral rite. The word *ritual*, however, is "the prescribed order of performing religious or other devotional service." This "prescribed order," which is followed in the ceremony, may be written down, so that ritual also can be understood as "a book containing the order, forms, or ceremonies, to be observed in the celebration of religious or other solemn service." So a funeral ceremony, or rite, puts into practice what the funeral ritual prescribes.

Defining the Christian Funeral

A Christian funeral is a ceremony connected with burying the body of a dead person, like funerals in other traditions, but the ceremony itself takes the form of Christian worship. This has implications for understanding how the funeral is a means of caring for the bereaved, so let's look more closely at its two main aspects, its worship and its connection with burial, before moving to liturgies.

Funeral Worship

According to James White, the word *worship* comes from an Old English word, *weorthscipe,* in which *weorth* means "worthy" and *scipe* means "ship." It signifies "attributing worth, or respect, to someone" (2000, 27). Christian worship involves ascribing worth, or respect, to God. White goes on to point out that several Greek words in the New Testament are commonly translated as "worship," but often they have other meanings also, which has the effect of bringing out different ways of characterizing worship. For instance, one such word, *latreia,* means "service" (27), as well as "worship," and another word translated as "worship," *proskunein,* connotes "falling down to show obeisance or prostration" (28).

Gordon Lathrop, in *Holy People: A Liturgical Ecclesiology,* develops an understanding of Christian worship that is helpful for learning how it can be an appropriate way to have a funeral ceremony. In the opening of his first chapter, he writes: "Assembly, a gathering together of participating persons, constitutes the most basic symbol of Christian worship. All the other symbols and symbolic actions of liturgy depend upon this gathering being there in the first place" (1999, 21). The Hebrew word for this assembly is *qahal,* and its Greek counterpart is *ekklesia.* It is God who calls the people to gather, so that they become the "the assembly of the people of God" (32).

According to Lathrop, this symbol of worship is eschatological, "for the ekklesia tradition also invites us to see that participation in this assembly is participation in Christian eschatology" (44). In accord with the symbol of assembly, Lathrop puts the traditional issue of concern with the last things in terms of the final assembly in which God is present. Current assemblies, all the local churches, and the larger church together practice assembling for worship, and by doing so, participate by faith in the promised final assembly on God's day. "Christian faith says that this assembly for which the biblical texts have caused us to hope–the *qahal*, the *ekklesia*–is actually taking place. According to that faith, the last-day assembly, in which God promises to begin to gather the nations around the holy Word, is as near as your local church" (73).

Because it is eschatological, assembly also symbolizes hope. Lathrop shows that the hope associated with assembly has deep roots in the Hebrew Scriptures and involves not only "hope for God to come" (33) but ultimately "hope for an end to violence and death as all people begin to be called into such an assembly before God" (33). He then argues that when Christians began using the word *assembly* for their gatherings, "most likely" (33) it symbolized this hope, a hope that had become related to Christ seen as its first fruits. "Against all appearances, Christians believed, God's final times have dawned in Jesus Christ, in his cross, his resurrection, and the faith which is through him" (33).

Another characteristic of Christian worship symbolized by assembly is truth. Lathrop says, "The texts and the actions of our liturgies...will show us that we are here as before God's own face. Those texts and actions will also seek to tell the truth about us and our world. The sense will be that there must be more to time and to life, since, to tell the truth, the world is both so beautiful and so full of evil, death, and sorrow" (44). Like hope, truth is related to Christ in worship.

> But for Christians, the truth includes this: Jesus Christ, the crucified and risen one, is the beginning of God's "more." He is the meaning of the world itself, before God. In the power of the Spirit of God, this assembly will then be made a community around him, as he is present in Scripture and in the breaking of bread. (44)

Finally, Lathrop relates assembly, the most basic symbol of Christian worship, to all that happens in worship.

> The symbol means something in the practice of assembly, in the exercise of those central things that belong to assembly, in the experience of juxtaposing word, table, bath, prayer, and song to our conceptions of meeting. Those things invite, persuade, enable our gatherings to be understood as gatherings around the resurrection of Jesus Christ, in the power of the Spirit, before the face of God, for the sake of the world. And these gatherings are called "church." (48)

A Christian funeral is such an assembly, a gathering "around the resurrection of Jesus Christ." Those who assemble for the funeral are placing themselves in relation to Christ in the sense of participating in worship that affirms the truth of Christ, seen as "the meaning of the world itself, before God." And, most importantly, they are participating in the hope that has "dawned in Jesus Christ, in his cross, his resurrection, and the faith which is through him." This contrasts with any view that says the participants must explicitly hear this or that said about the crucified and risen Christ in the funeral if they are to be presented with the message of hope. Also, attempts to draw psychotherapeutic benefits of the funeral are paltry in comparison.

The Funeral and Burial

Now we come to the second aspect of a Christian funeral. If assembly is to provide an adequate symbol for the worship occurring in a Christian funeral, it must take account of the fact that such a funeral is connected with burying the body of a dead person. Most often, the body is present in a casket, and the participants are mourners. The funeral normally concludes with a committal service at the cemetery, though the committal sometimes happens before the funeral worship.

Those who mourn the loss of the deceased are invited to assemble for worship in the funeral so that they can partake of the truth and hope that Christian worship affirms. This truth is about the real world as it exists before God, including our suffering related to death and grief. We do not just bring our suffering to worship in the abstract; we bring the real, concrete suffering we are experiencing as we assemble for worship, even when this suffering takes the form of grief and the realization of finitude. Nor do we just participate in hope in the abstract. The hope dawning in Christ speaks to our real situation, in this case our suffering related to the loss of a loved one.

Assembling for a Christian funeral and participating in it may include remembering the deceased, which is part of relating to the burial. This is the memorializing part of the funeral in which family or friends may speak about the deceased, sharing some memory of the person, giving thanks for the person, or reading a poem or letter. This is not done in every Christian funeral, but it may be done, and denominations vary in their approach to it. Remembering the deceased has, from time to time, been portrayed as something that competes with worshiping God in the funeral, by setting up a tension between a focus on God versus a focus on the deceased. Yet, this tension is false in a Christian funeral. Remembering the deceased goes hand in hand with the private thoughts of the mourners and may be part of what is done when people assemble for funerals. Whether in private thought or in speaking, remembering occurs in the context of the mourners' participation in the truth and hope of Christ. This remembering happens in the flow of the service amidst readings of scripture, singing hymns, and praying. It is not something that becomes a substitute, or competition, for these things.

The mourners who assemble for the funeral may be a very diverse group. Even when the deceased was a church member, many who attend the funeral may not be members of that congregation. Other denominations, and even other religions, may be represented among the mourners. Some may claim to be religious, but have no church affiliation, and some may claim not to be religious. Those who die do not have relationships only with church members.

A Christian funeral is open to all who want to attend, which does not compromise its integrity as worship. As Lathrop says, "Because of Jesus Christ, surprisingly, sinners and outsiders and Gentiles have been called into the assembly of God" (1999, 33). Christian worship always should convey openness to strangers, especially in funerals.

Within this openness, sensitivity and latitude are called for sometimes. For instance, a minister was talking to a bereaved family about the approaching funeral, when one family member asked him to please talk about love rather than God in the funeral. Certain nonreligious people were going to attend, and the family member did not want them to be offended. The minister agreed that, yes, God is love and that we can understand the implicit reference to God when speaking of love. Then, after pausing thoughtfully for a moment, he suggested that perhaps the deceased should be taken into account in considering this request. He then wondered aloud if the dead person would have wanted God to be mentioned, to which the spouse of the deceased immediately responded, "That's right!" This showed that the one family member did not represent the views of all the family members, affording the minister the opportunity to gently resist the request. When the minister attended the visitation on the following evening and approached the open casket, he observed a small copy of the New Testament resting in the hand of the deceased.

Sensitivity to a diverse group of mourners is consistent with a Christian funeral. Yet, it does not require hiding who you really are and what you really are doing. A mourner who is not religious may know quite well that the deceased was a Christian, as well as a member of a particular congregation, and fully expects the funeral to be in the religious tradition of the deceased. There also may be other complications. For instance, if the deceased was not religious, the family members may be church members in your congregation or another church and want an explicitly Christian funeral that nevertheless is sensitive to the nonbelief of the deceased. If the funeral liturgy is flexible, most situations of this sort can be addressed fruitfully.

Introducing Funeral Liturgies

Liturgy is an intriguing word, steeped in the history of Christian worship and multifaceted in meaning. It comes from the Greek word *leitourgia,* which means "a work performed by the people for the benefit of others" (White, 2000, 26). In Western Christian worship, it indicates that those who assemble for worship take an active part in worship rather than being merely passive recipients of something done for them by a worship leader. According to James White, "Western Christians use 'liturgical' to apply to all forms of public worship of a participatory nature" (26).

If worship is performed actively, liturgy also prescribes how that performance should take place. Like ritual, specific liturgies associated with different Christian denominations have been written down, as a help to clergy and church members. Historically, these writings have been categorized as liturgical books, but now they are called service books. (*The New Westminster Dictionary of Liturgy and Worship* contains excellent historical articles on liturgical books, and on burial, in different Christian denominations.)

In most contemporary service books, the written liturgy contains the order of worship, words to be said or sung in worship, and directions for carrying out worship (White, 2000, 30). The directions are called rubrics and often are printed in red, which goes back to the ancient Greek root meaning of *rubric*–"red." In addition to containing the liturgies for Sundays throughout the year, the service books also contain liturgies for a variety of occasions, including the occasion of death.

As a rather extensive illustration of liturgical books and what they say about funeral liturgies, I would like to compare some of the funeral instructions in four Protestant service books. Your denomination may have a different service book, and, if so, you are invited to compare yours with the ones presented here. Or your religious tradition may not have a service book, in which case you are invited to bring your funeral custom into dialogue with what is presented here. You may be on the cutting edge of contemporary worship, and you tend to set denominational books up as straw dogs to knock down. In this instance, you are invited to do something different, which is to bring your contemporary, cutting-edge funeral liturgy into comparison with the ones presented here. The point is not to decide which one is right, but for you to get more in touch with preparing a funeral in your tradition through bringing yours into comparison with others.

One service book is the *Book of Common Worship,* published in 1993, used in the Presbyterian Church (USA) and the Cumberland Presbyterian

Church. The Presbyterians also publish supplemental funeral materials that can be helpful to those who conduct funerals. For instance, one Presbyterian funeral resource, *Study Guide to the Funeral, A Service of Witness to the Resurrection,* uses the case method of teaching for educational purposes. In addition, *Services of Remembrance: A Worship Resource,* by the Presbyterian AIDS Network, provides resources for funerals of those who have died from AIDS. Finally, *The Funeral: A Service of Witness to the Resurrection, The Worship of God, Supplemental Liturgical Resource 4,* published in 1986, was used as a resource for developing the 1993 version of the *Book of Common Worship.* It contains funeral resources and commentary.

The second service book on which I will be drawing is the *Lutheran Book of Worship: Ministers Desk Edition,* published in 1978, used in most Lutheran congregations. This will be supplemented by *Occasional Services: A Companion to Lutheran Book of Worship,* published in 1982, because the two together contain what the other three service books provide in one book. In addition, *Commentary on the Lutheran Book of Worship: Lutheran Liturgy in Its Ecumenical Context* provides helpful funeral commentary.

The third service book on which I will draw is *The Book of Common Prayer,* published in 1979, used in the Protestant Episcopal Church in the United States of America, commonly called the Episcopal Church, USA. The Episcopal service book contains two funeral rites and also the brief outline of a third for times when neither the first nor second fits the situation. I will be using the second Episcopal funeral liturgy, called "Burial of the Dead: Rite Two." One supplemental Episcopal book is *Enriching Our Worship 2: Ministry with the Sick or Dying, Burial of a Child* (2000). As the subtitle indicates, it contains a funeral service for the burial of a child.

The final service book on which I will draw is the *United Methodist Book of Worship,* published in 1992, used in the United Methodist Church. A helpful United Methodist funeral resource is *A Service of Death and Resurrection: The Ministry of the Church at Death, Supplemental Worship Resources 7.* Among other things, it contains a discussion of ministry at the time of death and commentary on funerals.

Within the four service books, there are resources for use at the time of a death in addition to the funeral liturgy, such as prayers. Moreover, the four service books provide brief services for use with a gathering of family and friends of the deceased following the death but before the funeral. The service books also provide options within the funeral liturgy for use in different circumstances, such as the death of a child and sudden death. The United Methodist service book goes the extra mile by providing a separate funeral liturgy for a child who is stillborn, as opposed to incorporating that circumstance into the main funeral liturgy. These different circumstances will be noted within the discussion of the four funeral liturgies.

The comparison of funeral liturgies has four parts. In the rest of this chapter, I will focus on the rubrics, or directions, that guide the minister through the funeral. The rubrics are especially helpful when a minister is preparing a funeral service. In the next chapter, the four orders of worship will be compared, the words and music comprising the content of the four funerals will be compared, and the four committal services conducted at the cemetery will be compared. The discussion of the four funeral liturgies will be illustrative and in no way exhaustive.

Funeral Directions, or Rubrics

You may wonder: Why bother with directions? The answer is simple. If you must conduct funerals in the context of your denomination, you could not have a more helpful guide than the rubrics, especially when you are faced with conducting a funeral without much time to prepare it. Also, you are encouraged to examine the funeral directions provided by your denomination, whether written down, passed on through custom, or still in development, in order to bring them into dialogue with the historic ones presented here as a way of learning from them, and ultimately from yours.

Introductory Rubrics

In the four service books, introductory rubrics precede the funeral service, and some of the instructions found in the four books are identical except for slight variations in wording. For instance, the service books emphasize having the funeral in the church when the deceased was a church member:

Presbyterian: "Except for compelling reasons, the service for a believing Christian is normally held in the church, at a time when the congregation can be present" (911).

United Methodist: "[The funeral] should be held in the church if at all possible and at a time when members of the congregation can be present" (139).

Episcopal: "Baptized Christians are properly buried from the church. The service should be held at a time when the congregation has opportunity to be present" (490).

The Lutheran service book differs slightly: "The service is intended primarily for use in church with the body of the deceased present" (37).

At the same time, the four funeral liturgies are meant to be adapted for use in locations other than the church. As it says in the Lutheran service book, "Modifications of the service enable its use in other locations—crematory chapel, private house, funeral parlor—where processions and other liturgical actions are not feasible" (37). This is one kind of adaptability the funeral liturgies have, but not the only one.

Another kind of adaptability involves different circumstances in which the funeral liturgies may be used. The United Methodist service book identifies different names for the funeral when it is adapted to different circumstances relating to the presence or absence of the body in the service. "Funeral" is an appropriate name "for a service with the body of the deceased present." "Burial of the Dead" is appropriate "where the remains of the deceased are buried." "Memorial Service" is "appropriate when the body of the deceased is not present" (139).

Yet, this service book goes on to give the funeral a different name, "A Service of Death and Resurrection." This name is meant to be so broad that it can be used to cover all the different circumstances relating to the funeral service. More importantly, however, this name is related to an understanding of funerals as worship: "It expresses clearly the twofold nature of what is done: the facts of death and bereavement are honestly faced, and the gospel of resurrection is celebrated in the context of God's Baptismal Covenant with us in Christ" (139). Finally, the United Methodist service book instructs the minister: "When circumstances make the service as it stands inappropriate, the pastor may make adaptations...Ethnic and cultural traditions are encouraged and may be incorporated into the service at the discretion of the pastor"(139).

The other three service books also have their names for the funeral. The Presbyterian service book calls the funeral "A Service of Witness to the Resurrection" and gives the direction that "it may be adapted as a memorial service" (911). In the Lutheran service book, the funeral is named "Burial of the Dead," and it, too, "may be used as a memorial service" (331). Its introductory instructions discuss several different circumstances in which there may be a memorial service, for instance, when the body is to be transported to a distant interment site, when the body has been willed for medical research, or when the body is cremated (37). Likewise, in the Episcopal service book the funeral is called "The Burial of the Dead," but the designation "Rite Two" is added (490). Its introductory instructions do not address memorial services explicitly. However, following the brief third funeral outline, it does provide an explanation of funerals:

> The liturgy for the dead is an Easter liturgy. It finds all its meaning in the resurrection. Because Jesus was raised from the dead, we, too, shall be raised...The liturgy, therefore, is characterized by joy...This joy, however, does not make human grief unchristian...The very love we have for each other in Christ brings deep sorrow when we are parted by death...while we rejoice that one we love has entered into the nearer presence of our Lord, we sorrow in sympathy with those who mourn. (507)

One limit to adaptability involves societal organizations to which the deceased belonged. None of the service books allow ceremonies from these organizations to be mixed with the funeral worship service. For instance, the Presbyterian service book directs, "The ceremonies and rites of fraternal, civic, or military organizations, if any, should occur at some other time and place" (911). The Lutheran rubric is similar, but the Episcopal introductory directions do not mention this issue. The United Methodist service book takes greater account of the situation:

> If the family requests that there be military, fraternal, or other rites in addition to the Service of Death and Resurrection, the pastor should plan carefully the sequence and interrelationship of these services so that the service is not interrupted with other rites, and so that its integrity is supported and not compromised. (140)

There are additional introductory rubrics in each of the four service books, some similar, others different, because they address procedures unique to their denomination. For instance, unlike the other service books, the Lutheran book discusses candles and torches and their use in the processional at the beginning of the funeral. On the whole, however, similarities outweigh the differences.

Rubrics within the Funeral Order of Worship

Following the introductory rubrics, the four service books provide directions addressing each part of the funeral from beginning to end. These rubrics show the flexibility of the funeral liturgies. A flexible and adaptable funeral increases the likelihood that the funeral will provide a higher quality of care than would be possible otherwise.

If the minister has options, it is easier to adapt the funeral to different bereavement situations and funeral locations. The four service books give numerous options throughout the funeral in several ways. One is by allowing the minister to omit a part of the funeral liturgy that would be inappropriate at some locations. Another is by providing several alternatives in the content of the funeral. For instance, alternative prayers are often printed out, numerous suggestions for scripture readings are given and options for music are numerous. Rubrics point out these alternatives along the way in the liturgy.

Other options are addressed with the help of the word "may," which is used often in the rubrics. For instance, the rubrics in the four service books tell the minister that a pall may be placed over the coffin before the funeral begins, or it may be omitted, though there are differing emphases depending on the denomination. The pall is a white cloth containing the symbol of the cross, representing baptism. A hymn may be sung at a certain point in the service, or an alternative, such as a psalm, may be chosen. A certain type of prayer may be said, such as a prayer of confession, or it may be omitted. One prayer may be substituted for another depending on the circumstance, such as the death of a child or a sudden death. Communion may be served, or it may be omitted.

Two particularly significant options involve rubrics instructing the minister about mentioning the deceased and about involving others in the funeral, either for the purpose of speaking about the deceased or for assisting in the liturgy. The Presbyterian service book addresses this in two rubrics. In the introductory directions, this service book says, "Family members, friends, or members of the congregation may be invited by the minister to share in the service" (911). Then the rubric at the sermon in the order of worship says, "After the scriptures are read, their message may be proclaimed in a brief sermon. Expressions of gratitude to God for the life of the deceased may follow" (920).

The Lutheran service book, too, addresses this issue in introductory rubrics, in which the sermon is discussed: "The sermon is a proclamation of hope and comfort in Christ, but it may include appropriate recognition of the life of the deceased" (38). The second part of this rubric addresses other speakers: "It may be appropriate for relatives or associates of the deceased to comment briefly on the meaning of his or her life for them or in the community" (38).

The United Methodist service book says the most about involving others for remembering the deceased. The rubric given at the sermon says, "A sermon may be preached, proclaiming the gospel in the face of death. It may lead into, or include, the following acts of naming and witness" (149). Naming follows the sermon in the order of worship. Its rubric says, "The life and death of the deceased may be gathered up in the reading of a memorial or appropriate statement, or in other ways, by the pastor or others" (149). Witness follows naming. According to its rubric,

> Pastor, family, friends, and members of the congregation may briefly voice their thankfulness to God for the grace they have received in the life of the deceased and their Christian faith and joy. A poem or other reading such as *If Death My Friend and Me Divide*...may be read as a witness. Signs of faith, hope, and love may be exchanged. (149)

The Episcopal service book does not have similar rubrics, but it does encourage laypersons to read scripture in the funeral. One introductory direction says, "It is desirable that the Lesson from the Old Testament, and the Epistle, be read by lay persons" (490). It also allows a layperson to preside at the funeral: "When the services of a priest cannot be obtained, a deacon or lay reader may preside at the service" (490).

Finally, be aware that rubrics permeate the funeral orders of worship to be discussed in the next chapter. Otherwise, you inadvertently may assume that they are far more rigid, inflexible and inadaptable than they are in reality. For instance, the funeral order of worship in the Presbyterian service book begins with the placing of the pall (911). If you read this without awareness of the rubrics, you may assume that a pall always is placed over the coffin in a Presbyterian funeral. If you read the rubrics, however, you find out that the pall is optional, though family and friends who carry the coffin in the procession are called pallbearers whether or not the pall is used. So keep the rubrics in mind as you read the funeral orders of worship in the next chapter. In addition, note that the service books use the term *coffin,* though *casket* is more common today. (See Noren, 2001, 305 and 306 for definitions of casket and coffin.)

Conclusion

Christian funerals share something with non-Christian funerals–the very fact that they are funerals. In this regard, Christian funerals are by no means unique. Yet, they are distinct in the sense that they have the form of Christian worship, in which, as we have seen, the symbol of assembly is fundamental. Within Christianity, there are different liturgical traditions, each having its own funeral liturgy. As the liturgical comparison has shown, however, similarities between some differing traditions far outweigh the differences, which tend to be minor, and they are more adaptable and flexible than might be imagined. In the next chapter, the exploration of funeral liturgies will continue.

CHAPTER SEVEN

Preparing a Funeral Liturgy

This chapter is about the order of worship and the content that the minister prepares for the funeral, including the committal. Hopefully, this exploration will be helpful, but not in the way you might expect. Rather than suggesting one funeral order of worship containing a particular content, I will be comparing the funeral liturgies of the four denominations discussed in the last chapter. Ministers do not make up funeral liturgies; they draw on the worship resources provided by their denomination, whether the resources are written down in an official denominational book, are an unwritten part of a church's custom, or are associated with contemporary worship.

Given the huge diversity of religious traditions and local customs, not to mention the related diversity associated with different cultures, races, and ethnicities, the comparison in this chapter will be very limited and largely illustrative. Nevertheless, it can be helpful by encouraging you to examine the funeral liturgy of your denomination, or religious tradition. If your denomination is not included in this chapter, you are invited to add your funeral liturgy to the comparison.

Funeral Orders of Worship

Whatever else you do when preparing a funeral, you need to know how you are going to begin, what you are going to do next, and how you are going to end the funeral. In this section, the funeral order of worship will be explored through comparing the funeral orders of worship found in the four service books introduced in the previous chapter:

The *Book of Common Worship* used in the Presbyterian Church (USA) and in the Cumberland Presbyterian Church

The Book of Common Prayer used in the Episcopal Church, USA

The United Methodist Book of Worship used in the United Methodist Church

The *Lutheran Book of Worship: Ministers Desk Edition* is used in most Lutheran congregations. It will be supplemented with *Occasional Services: A Companion to Lutheran Book of Worship*.

Book of Common Worship
"The Funeral: A Service of Witness to the Resurrection" (910, 911–38)

Placing of the Pall (pall may be placed on coffin before procession)
Sentences of Scripture (or hymn or psalm sung during procession)
Psalm, Hymn, or Spiritual (may be sung)
Prayer
(Confession and Pardon may follow)
Prayer for Illumination
Old Testament, New Testament, Gospel Readings (psalm or canticle
  may be sung or read between the scripture readings)
Sermon
Affirmation of Faith (Apostles' Creed or other options given)
Hymn
Prayers of Thanksgiving, Supplication, and Intercession
Communion may be served
Lord's Prayer
Commendation (may be preceded by a hymn)
Blessing (serves as dismissal)
Procession (hymn, or psalm or canticle may be sung or said, pall
  removed after procession)

The Book of Common Prayer
"The Burial of the Dead: Rite Two" (491–500)

Anthem (or hymn, or psalm sung or said)
(Introductory words)
Collect
Additional Prayer (may follow Collect)
Old Testament (psalm, hymn, or canticle may follow)
New Testament (psalm, hymn, or canticle may follow)
The Gospel
Homily
Apostles' Creed
Lord's Prayer
Prayers of the People
Communion may be served
The Commendation (may be preceded by a hymn, or anthem sung
  or said)
Blessing and Dismissal
Procession (hymn or anthem or canticle may be sung or said)

The United Methodist Book of Worship
"A Service of Death and Resurrection" (139–54)

Gathering (hymns may be sung; pall may be placed on coffin)
The Word of Grace (procession)
Greeting (introductory words)
Hymn or Song
Prayer
Psalm 130 (may be sung or spoken)
Old Testament Lesson
Psalm 23 (may be sung or spoken)
New Testament Lesson
Psalm, Canticle, or Hymn (recommended here or after the Old
   Testament Lesson)
Gospel Lesson
Sermon
Naming (a memorial statement)
Witness (statement of thanks)
Hymn or Song
Creed or Affirmation of Faith (hymn or other music may precede
   or follow)
Prayer
Commendation
Communion may be served
Prayer of Thanksgiving
Lord's Prayer
Hymn (may be sung during recessional)
Dismissal with Blessing

Lutheran Book of Worship, Ministers Desk Edition
"Burial of the Dead" (331–36)

Entrance (pall may be placed on coffin, gather for procession)
Procession (psalm, hymn, or verse may be sung)
Prayer
Old Testament Lesson
(psalm, hymn, or verse may be sung between scripture readings)
New Testament Lesson
Verse (may be sung before Gospel is read)
Gospel
Sermon
Hymn
Apostles' Creed
Prayers
Communion may be served

Lord's Prayer
Commendation
Dismissal
Procession (psalm, hymn, or anthem may be sung)

The four funeral orders of worship are very similar. The procession, music and prayer quickly lead to scripture readings, including Old Testament, New Testament, and Gospel readings. In addition, all allow for hymns and other liturgical songs to be sung, or in some instances said, between the readings. Next comes the sermon following the scripture readings. Then, following the sermon, come a creed, prayers, the Lord's Prayer, the option of celebrating communion, and the commendation. The funerals end with a dismissal and a procession.

Differences are minor. For instance, the United Methodist order of worship includes the Naming and Witness after the sermon, unlike the others. Otherwise, the main differences have to do with slight variations in the orders of worship, such as where the Lord's Prayer is placed. Communion also has variations in placement.

Words Said and Sung in Funerals

Comparing the content of the four funeral liturgies potentially is a massive project, so this section will be the most illustrative in the comparison. The parts of the funeral to be compared are music, prayers, scripture readings, sermons, and commendations. Just as rubrics in the funeral liturgies provide flexibility by giving ministers options for adapting funerals to different circumstances, the content of the funeral liturgies in the service books also provides flexibility and adaptability through options.

Music

In its introductory rubrics, the Lutheran service book includes a brief discussion of music at funerals. It says that, in general, music at a funeral should "reflect the spirit of Christian confidence, trust, and hope in the resurrection characteristic of the spoken parts of the service." More specifically, in addition to hope in the resurrection, hymns should reflect "such themes as invocation of the Holy Spirit, comfort, the communion of saints." Finally, it emphasizes high quality, performers playing or singing within the bounds of their abilities, and avoidance of triteness and sentimentality that would cloud communication of the content and mood of the service (39).

The four funeral orders of worship include music at the beginning of the funeral, such as during the procession. Next, they include it between scripture readings, then at some point after the sermon, and finally at the end of the funeral. One choice the person preparing the funeral has to make involves the type of music to sing. There are hymns; psalms set to music, or the Psalter; and liturgical songs containing biblical lyrics, called canticles, anthems, or verses. Except for hymns, these other types require the additional choice of whether to say or sing them.

For instance, the Episcopal funeral liturgy begins with a choice of saying or singing one or more of five anthems printed out. The first one is from John 11:25–26, in which Jesus is talking to Martha after the death of Lazarus: "I am Resurrection and I am Life, says the Lord. Whoever has faith in me shall have life, even though he die. And everyone who has life, and has committed himself to me in faith, shall not die for ever" (491). In the Lutheran equivalent, three optional verses are listed for singing in the procession (190). The United Methodist service book prints out the equivalent of Episcopal anthems under the "Word of Grace" in the order of worship, but this word is said, not sung. The equivalent in the Presbyterian service book is under the "Sentences of Scripture" in the order of worship, including nineteen passages printed out. Normally, this scripture is said, but it may be sung during the procession.

Occasional Services: A Companion to Lutheran Book of Worship contains psalms printed out in the order of worship that may be sung between the scripture readings, including Psalm 46:1–7 and Psalm 121 (116–17). Four such psalms are listed in the *Lutheran Book of Worship: Ministers Desk Edition* but are not printed out (190). The Episcopal service book lists psalms for singing after the scripture readings, but only prints them out in "Rite One." In the United Methodist service book, Psalms 130 and 23 are printed out in the order of worship and may be sung or said. The Presbyterian service book lists psalms for singing between scripture readings (948) and refers to psalms printed out in another section (611–783).

The United Methodist service book (160–61) lists twenty-eight hymns found in *The United Methodist Hymnal,* which includes a wide variety, from "The Church's One Foundation" to "Leaning on the Everlasting Arms." In addition, this service book refers to four different sections of that hymnal, including "Death and Eternal Life," "Communion of the Saints," "Eternal Life and Funerals," and "Memorial Services." The Presbyterian service book (920) refers to the *Presbyterian Hymnal* at one point in the funeral liturgy, but there are no hymns listed.

Hymn choices are as broad as denominational hymnals or other hymnals or hymns used. Special music, as well as hymns, can be requested by the bereaved family (see Noren, 2001, 265–81, for an excellent selection of hymns and other musical resources for funerals).

First Prayer

Two main places for prayer are found in the four funeral liturgies. The first place is just before the scripture readings, and the second is after the sermon, creed, and music. Like suggested content in other parts of the four funeral liturgies, many of these prayers are very similar, and some are the same. They are meant to be a help to ministers and may be used as they are, tailored to specific circumstances, or reflected upon to inspire the writing of similar prayers. I have included different prayers from the four funeral books for both the first and second prayers. The first prayer is discussed here, and the second prayer is discussed after the section on the sermon.

The United Methodist service book prints out three optional prayers for possible use at this point in the service. One focuses on petition for God's help:

> O God, who gave us birth, you are ever more ready to hear than
>   we are to pray.
> You know our needs before we ask, and our ignorance in asking.
> Give to us now your grace, that as we shrink before the mystery of
>   death, we may see the light of eternity.
> Speak to us once more your solemn message of life and of death.
> Help us to live as those who are prepared to die.
> And when our days here are accomplished, enable us to die as
>   those who go forth to live, so that living or dying, our life may
>   be in you, and that nothing in life or in death will be able to
>   separate us from your great love in Christ Jesus our Lord. Amen.
>   (142–43)

The second optional prayer gives thanksgiving for those who have died previously and then expresses thanks for the person for whom the funeral is being held: "Especially we praise you for *Name,* whom you have graciously received into your presence" (143). The third prayer, which may follow either of the first two, is a prayer of confession followed by an assurance of pardon. Finally, in a separate section, this service book provides additional funeral prayers: "for general use"; "at the service for a child"; "for an untimely or tragic death"; and "at the service for a person who did not profess the Christian faith" (158–66).

The Presbyterian service book prints out five optional prayers for possible use at this early point in the funeral. One expresses praise to each person of the Trinity:

> Eternal God, maker of heaven and earth:
> You formed us from the dust of the earth, and by your breath you
>   gave us life.
> We glorify you.
> Jesus Christ, the resurrection and the life:
> You tasted death for all humanity,
>   and by rising from the grave you opened the way to eternal life.

We praise you.
Holy spirit, author and giver of life:
You are the comforter of all who sorrow,
    our sure confidence and everlasting hope.
We worship you.
To you, O blessed Trinity, be glory and honor, forever and ever.
    Amen. (915–16)

The second and third prayers are the same as the first two in the United Methodist service book, and the fourth prayer is a petition for help in light of human finitude: "Eternal God, we acknowledge the uncertainty of our life on earth...Turn your ear to our cry, and hear our prayer" (917). The final prayer is an optional prayer of confession followed by an assurance of pardon.

The Lutheran service book contains five optional prayers printed out for use before the scripture readings. The first names the deceased, giving thanks for the person, and goes on to ask God for help in mourning and living in the knowledge of death. The second petitions God for help in mourning: "Almighty God...deal graciously, we pray, with those who mourn" (332). The third gives thanks for "your servants who have finished their course in faith and now rest from their labors" (332). The fourth prayer, like the fourth prayer in the Presbyterian service book, is a petition for help in light of human finitude.

The final prayer is for use in the funeral of a child: "O God our Father, your beloved Son took children into his arms and blessed them. Give us grace, we pray, that we may entrust *(name)* to your never-failing care and love, and bring us all to your heavenly kingdom; through your Son, Jesus Christ our Lord" (333).

In the Episcopal service book, three optional collects are printed out for an adult burial, and all three mention the deceased by name. For instance, the first one says: "O God, who by the glorious resurrection of your Son Jesus Christ destroyed death, and brought life and immortality to light: Grant that your servant N., being raised with him, may know the strength of his presence, and rejoice in his eternal glory" (493).

An additional collect is provided for use at the burial of a child. Finally, another prayer that may follow the collect is printed out. It is a prayer for the mourners in their grief.

Scripture Readings or Lessons

If each service book contained one Old Testament lesson, one New Testament lesson, and one gospel reading, and these readings were required, comparison would be easy. However, reality is more complicated. The four service books contain whole lists of suggested biblical passages, with some printed out, either within the funeral order of worship or in a separate section. These suggestions are meant to be a help to the minister, who is free to use any passage from scripture in the funeral. As an example, consider the suggested lists for the Old Testament lesson in the four service books.

In the Episcopal service book (494), the following suggested readings are listed: Isaiah 25:6–9; Isaiah 61:1–3; Lamentations 3:22–26, 31–33; Job 19:21–27a; and an apocryphal passage, Wisdom 3:1–5, 9. The Lutheran service book (191) lists the same four passages, except for starting with verse 23 in the Job passage, but leaves out the apocryphal passage. It also suggests that the Lamentations passage is appropriate for use at the burial of a child. *Occasional Services: A Companion to Lutheran Book of Worship* (128) lists the same passages and also prints out Job 19:23–27a and Isaiah 25:6–9 in the funeral order of worship (116).

The Presbyterian service book (947–63), in a section following the committal, lists the same Old Testament readings and apocryphal passage suggested in the Episcopal service book, some being the exact same verses, but several including additional verses, such as Isaiah 61:1–4, 10–11, rather than Isaiah 61:1–3. It also lists seven additional passages from Isaiah, as well as a passage from Daniel and one from Joel. Finally, it lists Old Testament passages for two special circumstances. One is "at the loss of a child" (948), including Zechariah 8:1–8 and Isaiah 65:17–25. The other circumstance is "for those whose faith is unknown" (948), including Ecclesiastes 3:1–15 and Lamentations 3:1–9, 19–23. Six of the Old Testament passages are printed out in the service book, as well as listed.

Like the Lutheran service book, the United Methodist service book lists the same Old Testament readings as the Episcopal service book except for the apocryphal passage. The two Isaiah passages and the Job passage are part of a list containing nineteen Old Testament readings, found in the section on additional funeral resources following the committal service (158–69). The Lamentations passage is in a different list under resources for the funeral service of a child (162). In addition to this special circumstance, the United Methodist service book also suggests Old Testament readings "for an untimely or tragic death" (164) and "at the service for a person who did not profess the Christian faith" (166). Within the funeral order of worship, Isaiah 40:1–8 and 40:28–31 are printed out, followed by three additional passages listed, two from Isaiah and one from Exodus.

In the four service books, the New Testament reading and the reading of the gospel lesson provide the same flexible options as the Old Testament reading. There are many suggested readings listed, and some are printed out. Some readings are the same in each service book, but the Presbyterian and United Methodist service books contain larger lists than the Episcopal and Lutheran service books.

Sermons

Because the content of sermons is not included in the service books, these books say relatively little about funeral sermons. What they do say is found in the rubrics:

The Presbyterian service book says: "After the scriptures are read, their message may be proclaimed in a brief sermon. Expressions of gratitude to God for the life of the deceased may follow" (920).

The United Methodist service book says: "A sermon may be preached, proclaiming the gospel in the face of death. It may lead into, or include, the following acts of naming and witness" (149).

The Lutheran service book says: "The sermon will usually be a part of the service, though, where circumstances suggest it, it may be omitted. The sermon is a proclamation of hope and comfort in Christ, but it may include appropriate recognition of the life of the deceased" (38).

The Episcopal service book says: "Here there may be a homily by the Celebrant, or a member of the family, or a friend" (495).

The Presbyterian and United Methodist sermon rubrics include a suggested movement beginning with proclaiming the gospel and then moving toward the life of the deceased. The Lutheran service book, too, includes a focus on proclaiming the gospel and mentioning the life of the deceased but also acknowledges that there are times when the sermon may need to be omitted, though it does not mention what such circumstances may be. The Episcopal rubric is the most sparse of the four, but it brings out the possibility of someone other than the minister preaching the sermon. Overall, it should be noted, as it was in the previous chapter, that mentioning the life of the deceased, either in the context of the sermon itself or immediately following the sermon, is appropriate in a Christian funeral.

Second Prayer

The second main place for prayer in the four funeral liturgies is after the sermon, creed, and music. It is an intercessory prayer said in conjunction with the Lord's Prayer and with the commendation.

In the United Methodist service book, this second prayer may take the form of "a pastoral prayer, a series of shorter prayers, or a litany" (149). Whatever its form, however, it is a prayer of intercession for the mourners. Here is the one printed in the order of worship:

> God of us all, your love never ends.
> When all else fails, you still are God.
> We pray to you for one another in our need, and for all, anywhere,
>   who mourn with us this day.
> To those who doubt, give light;
> To those who are weak, strength;

To all who have sinned, mercy;
To all who sorrow, your peace.
Keep true in us the love with which we hold one another.
In all our ways we trust you.
And to you, with your Church on earth and in heaven,
We offer honor and glory, now and for ever. Amen. (149–50)

The commendation comes right after this prayer. In turn, a prayer of thanksgiving, in which God is praised, follows the commendation and leads into the Lord's Prayer.

In the Presbyterian service book, the second prayer is under the title, "Prayers of Thanksgiving, Supplication, and Intercession" (921–24, additional prayers on 907–8). Seven optional prayers are printed, including one in the form of a litany. The fifth and sixth are "at the death of a child" (923), and the seventh is for use "after a sudden death"(924). Here is the prayer addressing sudden death:

God of compassion,
comfort us with the great power of your love
as we mourn the sudden death of N.
In our grief and confusion,
help us find peace in the knowledge of your loving mercy to all
    your children,
and give us light to guide us into the assurance of your love;
through Jesus Christ our Lord. Amen. (924)

The Lord's Prayer follows the prayer of intercession, and the commendation follows the Lord's Prayer, though these latter two may be separated by a hymn.

In the Lutheran service book, the prayer of intercession is in the form of a litany:

Assisting Minister: Let us pray. Almighty God, you have knit your chosen people together in one communion, in the mystical body of your Son, Jesus Christ our Lord.
Give to your whole Church in heaven and on earth your light and your peace.

Congregation: Hear us, Lord.

Assisting Minister: Grant that all who have been baptized into Christ's death and resurrection may die to sin and rise to newness of life and that through the grave and gate of death we may pass with him to our joyful resurrection.

Congregation: Hear us, Lord.

Assisting Minister: Grant to us who are still in our pilgrimage, and who walk as yet by faith, that your Holy Spirit may lead us in holiness and righteousness all our days.

Congregation: Hear us, Lord.

Assisting Minister: Grant to your faithful people pardon and peace, that we may be cleansed from all our sins and serve you with a quiet mind.

Congregation: Hear us, Lord.

Assisting Minister: Grant to all who mourn a sure confidence in your loving care, that, casting all their sorrow on you, they may know the consolation of your love.

Congregation: Hear us, Lord

Assisting Minister: Give courage and faith to those who are bereaved, that they may have strength to meet the days ahead in the comfort of a holy and certain hope, and in the joyful expectation of eternal life with those they love.

Congregation: Hear us, Lord. (335)

Assisting Minister: Help us, we pray, in the midst of things we cannot understand, to believe and trust in the communion of saints, the forgiveness of sins, and the resurrection to life everlasting.

Congregation: Hear us, Lord.

Assisting Minister: Grant us grace to entrust *(name)* to your never-failing love which sustained *him/her* in this life. Receive *him/her* into the arms of your mercy, and remember *him/her* according to the favor you bear for your people.

Congregation: Hear us, Lord. (334–35)

A prayer of thanks to God, for which two options are printed, concludes the litany. Next is the Lord's Prayer, which is followed by the commendation.

Finally, in the Episcopal service book, the Lord's Prayer precedes the intercessory prayer, or "Prayers of the People" (496), unlike the other three funeral liturgies. Although a prayer in the form of a litany is printed, this form is to be used when there is communion (additional litanies are on 465 and 480). Eight optional prayers are printed in a separate section following the committal (503–5, and see 202, 253). One of the prayers says:

> Grant, O Lord, to all who are bereaved the spirit of faith and courage, that they may have strength to meet the days to come with steadfastness and patience; not sorrowing as those without hope, but in thankful remembrance of your great goodness, and in the joyful expectation of eternal life with those they love. And this we ask in the Name of Jesus Christ our Savior. Amen. (505)

The commendation, which may be preceded by music, follows the intercessory prayer when there is no communion.

Commendation

In the commendation, the minister recommends the deceased to God. The Lutheran and Episcopal service books instruct the minister to stand near the coffin when saying the commendation. The United Methodist service book gives the same instruction but also gives the option of laying hands on the coffin or urn as the commendation is said. The Presbyterian service book simply has the minister face the body.

All four service books contain the same historic commendation, quoted here from the Lutheran service book:

"Into your hands, O merciful Savior, we commend your servant, *(name)*. Acknowledge, we humbly beseech you, a sheep of your own fold, a lamb of your own flock, a sinner of your own redeeming. Receive *him/her* into the arms of your mercy, into the blessed rest of everlasting peace, and into the glorious company of the saints in light" (336).

Except for the United Methodist order of worship, which includes prayers and a hymn following the commendation, the dismissal and procession follow the commendation, which ends the funeral.

Committal Services

The committal service happens at the cemetery where the body is to be entombed in a grave or mausoleum, which is a building at the cemetery containing crypts in which caskets are placed. If ashes are to be buried instead of a body, the urn containing the ashes may be buried in a grave or columbarium, which is like a mausoleum for ashes. When ashes are not present at the funeral, and they are not to be buried, the funeral order of worship is adapted accordingly and is called a memorial service. This circumstance requires no committal.

The committal may occur prior to the funeral, or even at another time. Traditionally, and most often, it follows the funeral worship, which requires that the mourners drive to the cemetery. When the body is to be buried, the pallbearers carry the casket to the hearse right from the funeral worship, with the minister leading the way. This is an extension of the procession at the end of the service. Then the minister and mourners, the ones who choose to attend the committal, drive to the cemetery together in a funeral procession led by the hearse, which transports the body. When the procession of cars arrives at the cemetery, the pallbearers, again led by the minister, carry the casket to the burial site where the committal takes place. The funeral director guides the pallbearers throughout this process of carrying the casket to the hearse and then to the burial site. When ashes are to be buried, the mourners drive to the cemetery individually. The bereaved family can request that the committal be private, so that others who attend the funeral do not attend the committal, but this is not the norm.

In the four service books, the committal follows the funeral order of worship and contains its own set of helpful rubrics. As the committal services below reveal, these services are brief, and any differences between them are very minor.

Book of Common Worship

"The Committal" (939–46)

Scripture Sentences
Committal

"In sure and certain hope of the resurrection to eternal life, through our Lord Jesus Christ, we commend to almighty God our *brother/sister* N., and we commit *his/her* body to the ground, earth to earth, ashes to ashes, dust to dust.

Blessed are the dead who die in the Lord, says the Spirit. They rest from their labors, and their works follow them" (940).

(Revisions are given for burial at sea, at a cremation service, and at a columbarium)

Lord's Prayer
Prayers
Blessing

The Book of Common Prayer

"The Committal" (501–3)

The Consecration of a Grave (said at convenient time not at the
    committal)
Anthem
Committal

"In sure and certain hope of the resurrection to eternal life through our Lord Jesus Christ, we commend to Almighty God our *brother* N., and we commit *his* body to the ground; earth to earth, ashes to ashes, dust to dust. The Lord bless *him* and keep *him*, the Lord make his face to shine upon *him* and be gracious to *him*, the Lord lift up his countenance upon *him* and give *him* peace. *Amen*" (501).

(Revision is made for the deep, the elements, the resting place.)

Lord's Prayer
Prayer
Dismissal

The United Methodist Book of Worship

"A Service of Committal" (155–57)

Opening Sentences
Prayer
Scripture Reading
Committal

"Almighty God, into your hands we commend your *son/daughter Name*, in sure and certain hope of resurrection to eternal life through Jesus Christ our Lord. Amen.

This body we commit to the ground (*to the elements, to its resting place*), earth to earth, ashes to ashes, dust to dust.

Blessed are the dead who die in the Lord. Yes, says the Spirit, they will rest from their labors for their deeds follow them" (156).

Prayers
Lord's Prayer
Hymn
Dismissal with Blessing

Lutheran Book of Worship: Ministers Desk Edition
"Committal" (337–39)

Procession
Prayer
Scripture Lesson
Committal

"In sure and certain hope of the resurrection to eternal life through our Lord Jesus Christ, we commend to almighty God our *brother/sister, (name),* and we commit *his/her* body to *the ground/the deep/the elements/its resting place*; earth to earth, ashes to ashes, dust to dust. The Lord bless *him/her* and keep *him/her*. The Lord make his face shine on *him/her* and be gracious to *him/her*. The Lord look upon *him/her* with favor and give *him/her* peace" (338).

Lord's Prayer
Prayer
Blessing and Dismissal

The four service books include variations on the same historic committal statement. Though there are minor differences among them, they are far more alike than different.

At the end of the committal, the mourners may stand around talking, but the minister is not obligated to stay until everyone has gone. If there is to be a meal following the committal, the minister attends the meal with the mourners, going directly from the cemetery to the location of the meal which may be a restaurant, church, or home. The minister may be asked to say the blessing when the mourners have assembled for the meal and is free to leave and do other things at the end of the meal.

Conclusion

The four service books contain massive amounts of material to help ministers prepare funerals, including committal services. Their orders of worship and their content, as well as the rubrics, are flexible and adaptable in most instances. Perhaps yours is similar, or it may be very different. Either way, hopefully you are growing in awareness of the funeral liturgy in your tradition.

CHAPTER EIGHT

Funerals and Mourning

In chapter 6, we saw that Christian funerals share a similarity with all kinds of funerals, and they have a difference from all other funerals. The difference is that they take the form of Christian worship, which was addressed in chapters 6 and 7. The similarity is that a Christian funeral is a ceremony, or a rite, connected to burying the dead, like non-Christian funerals. In this chapter, I will focus on the similarity in order to show how a Christian funeral can provide the means of mourning for newly bereaved people during the first phase of grief. My reason for going in this direction is that it helps to explain how caring for the bereaved during the first phase of grief happens through funerals, because facilitating mourning is what pastoral care is all about during this time (see chapter 9). Such things as comforting are not excluded, but comforting is the subject of chapter 10.

Though I will be using the term *funeral* quite a bit, almost everything discussed also will apply to memorial services. In addition, the discussion will apply to the period beginning at the point of death and extending all the way through the funeral. This will be characterized as the time of funeral preparation, on the part of the bereaved, as well as the pastor; the visitation and the funeral service, which includes the committal; and the concluding meal if there is one.

In the first part of the chapter, mourning in the psychological understanding of grief will be explored. Next, mourning seen in relation to the funeral, when the funeral is viewed as a rite of passage, will be explored. Finally, the relationship of funerals, mourning, and grief will be explored.

Mourning

Normally, a funeral takes place during the first phase of grief, the avoidance phase, in which there is a quite natural desire to avoid the reality of the death that has occurred. As we saw in chapter 3, the avoidance phase of grief begins with shock, which may range from mild to extreme. Shock then gives way to denial, which usually is partial, so that grief in its psychological, behavioral, social, and physical dimensions may appear in any number of configurations at this point.

Mourning associated with this phase of grief addresses the death being avoided. This means that there are two opposing forces at work in newly bereaved people, one being the desire to avoid the reality of the death and the other being the need to face the reality of the death. Consequently, mourning must be a gentle counterforce against shock and denial. Funerals have to do with this mourning process, so let's look at it more closely.

Mourning in the Avoidance Phase of Grief

Recall from chapter 2 that the first mourning operation characterizes one goal of mourning, which is undoing psychosocial ties to the deceased. During this mourning operation, the bereaved person focuses on the deceased primarily, as opposed to the self or the world. Although this mourning operation cannot be confined to the initial avoidance phase of grief, it nevertheless begins there. Mourning at this time has the purpose of coming to grips with the death (Rando, 1993, 24), which is a necessary first step toward the larger goal of undoing psychosocial ties to the deceased.

The specific mourning process that provides the means of accomplishing this purpose of coming to grips with the death is the first of the six R processes discussed in chapter 2, which Rando calls Recognize the Loss (1993, 44). Recognizing the loss takes place in two ways, acknowledging the death and understanding the death (44–47). Let's look first at acknowledging the death and then at understanding it.

Acknowledging the Death

Acknowledging the reality of the death initially takes place on an intellectual level, "involving only recognition and concession of the fact of the death" (Rando, 1993, 44; also see 393–95). But this initial acknowledgment should not be overlooked, or dismissed as merely superficial, because it is a necessary first step toward the eventual acceptance of the death at a deeper emotional level, which occurs over time as the bereaved person experiences the grief process. Without acknowledgment, the bereaved person may "construe the loss as a temporary absence which, although causing sadness due to separation, does not demand the same type of reorientation and readaptation as does death" (44). As Rando points out, this is why such strenuous efforts are made to recover the body in cases where the death cannot be confirmed immediately, such as after an airplane crash or boating accident.

In the absence of sufficient evidence to confront mourners with the death...they can postpone their mourning or rationalize it away. A high percentage of mourners who experience complications either have not viewed the body or have failed to participate in funeral rituals. Nothing opposes their need to deny and avoid. (45–46)

I would like to emphasize the word *reality* in all of this. Even though the initial acknowledgment of the death may involve only the barest recognition and concession of the fact of the death, this acknowledgment nevertheless contains the seeds of the sense that the death is real. However, if only the seeds of death's reality are part of this initial bare acknowledgment, this also must leave room for a continuing sense of aliveness that will not go away immediately. This is why relating denial only to experiencing the emotions of grief is inadequate. Grasping the reality of the death is not merely an admission, as if the bereaved person had been lying and now confesses the truth. It involves a much more comprehensive psychological process in which the bereaved person experiences a changing perception of the deceased. Let me give an example from my own experience.

When I was in my early thirties, my grandfather, my mother's father, died. Following the funeral service and burial, the family, around twenty individuals, returned to the cemetery after the grave was filled in and the flowers had been arranged. For a good hour or so, we stood around talking as if at a family reunion. During this time, I had a sudden recognition that I had witnessed this scene before, in fact many times before. Every Thanksgiving and Christmas during the entire time I was growing up, I witnessed this family reunion scene at my grandparents' house. Now, it was as if the living room had shifted to the cemetery. This led to a second recognition, that my grandfather had been a lynchpin holding this part of my family together. Now, death had removed the linchpin, and the family never again would be held together in the same way. In one respect, this thought about my family could be viewed as the beginning of a secondary loss accompanying the death of my grandfather. Yet, it was more than this.

My family thoughts were tied up intimately with mourning the loss of my grandfather, which, as it turns out, precisely involved trying to grasp the reality of his death on that afternoon at the cemetery. Related to the moment of witnessing the family scene, I was experiencing a certain perception of my grandfather. I knew perfectly well that he was dead. Yet, alongside this awareness, and in spite of it, I also had an image of him being alive in a certain way. It was as if he was in a kind of peaceful sleep in his new home, the casket buried in the grave. The image of sleep does not really capture my sense of his newfound existence. Rather, it was a sense of his peaceful presence associated with his body in the casket. The family members were carrying on as they had done traditionally, only now we had shifted to the cemetery so that he would be present.

When we returned to my grandmother's house, my attention was drawn in other directions, and I did not continue having the same psychological sense of my grandfather's presence. But since that time, I have heard many bereavement stories from church members involving the sense of presence of lost loved ones. It helps me understand that making death real is not an easy notion (also see Parkes, 1972, 65–66). A focus on thoughts and feelings alone is inadequate for understanding the beginning of mourning. It is more like the tumblers of your being shifting into a new configuration so that you can consciously grasp the new reality of death, which includes the perception that the body is no longer alive. But it takes time for the shift to happen.

Understanding the Death

In addition to acknowledging the death, the bereaved person also needs to gain some understanding of the reasons for it. According to Rando, "these are not philosophical or religious reasons; rather, they concern the facts contributing to the death and the circumstances surrounding it" (1993, 46; also see 398). The reasons need to make sense to the bereaved person, even though others may disagree. For instance, Rando gives the example of a father who refused to accept that his son committed suicide and insisted instead that the death was an accident. Understanding reasons for the death of a loved one gives a meaningful context to it, helping the bereaved person avoid anxiety and confusion that accompany the inevitable "wondering about what happened to her loved one and what potentially could happen to her" if reasons are not known (46–47).

A pastor, in his first year at a new church, was asked to officiate at the funeral of an elderly church member who died. The woman who died had four adult children, who met with the pastor for funeral planning after they arrived from out of town. During this meeting, something came out that shows how important understanding the death can be in a given circumstance. The pastor learned that the adult children's father had committed suicide ten years earlier and that there was a serious problem related to this. The previous minister, who conducted the funeral, had told the children that suicide was a sin and that their father was going to hell. This had a powerful effect on them and affected their grief. Very likely, it made acknowledging the death even more difficult, on top of having to cope with the fact of suicide. Now, the new pastor had the opportunity to help them come to a better understanding of their father's death.

He told them his understanding that suicide results from an extremely serious form of depression, rather than being a sin punishable by eternal damnation. Although the father's death was tragic, it was not a block to God's accepting and redemptive love, and they should be free to grieve his loss. Finally, he apologized for what the former pastor said to them. None of the four children said much in response, which is understandable because they had been living with the terrible false assumption about their father for so long.

In the funeral sermon, the pastor preached about grace and how nothing is greater than God's love for redeeming us. Although the explicit focus was on the mother, it also was a subtle message to the children about their father. During the reception in the fellowship hall after the service, one of the adult children approached the pastor and said that today enabled him to finally let go of the former pastor's statement with which he had been living for so many years.

In this instance, understanding the death was tied up closely with theology and played an important role in the grief process of each adult child over a decade. It highlights the reality that understanding the death, as well as acknowledging it, cannot be divorced from funeral preparation or the funeral service during the avoidance phase of grief. It also highlights the weight of authority a pastor's words may carry during this time, as well as the potential impact that the words of well-meaning but misguided friends may have on the bereaved. This brings us to the funeral itself, seen in relation to mourning during the avoidance phase of grief.

One Way That Funerals Facilitate Mourning

Funeral preparation and the visitation followed by the funeral (or memorial) service provide the primary means by which people in our society mourn in the avoidance phase of grief. This is how newly bereaved human beings are helped to acknowledge the reality of a death, fight the complete dominance of their denial and begin undoing psychosocial ties to the deceased. In order to get a feel for the importance of funeral time and the funeral ceremony itself, imagine that there is no such thing as a funeral or memorial service. Instead, imagine for instance that when a person dies in a hospital, the hospital simply disposes of the body. The immediate family is called, but that's it. There is no need for the family to call a funeral home, or the minister, to make any funeral arrangements. Instead, everyone returns to work or school. It is business as usual, except for a conspicuous absence. In many instances, others would find out about the death only by accident after weeks or months.

It is clear that something is needed to help human beings counter the avoidance of death, and for better or worse, we use funerals for this purpose. The hospital does not do the most convenient thing, which would be to dispose of the body. Instead, there must be communication with family members and funeral homes so that the body can be prepared for the funeral. This takes human resources, time, and money. Businesses and schools allow bereaved family members time off so that they can attend the visitation and funeral. Ministers, church members, bereaved friends, colleagues of the deceased, and friends of the family rearrange their daily schedules so that they can attend the visitation and funeral. Funeral homes sometimes must make arrangements with the local police to manage traffic during a funeral procession to the cemetery. Laws allow for these processions. In other words, funerals require the cooperation of a community, including that of churches and pastors.

The entire process, beginning at the point of death and not completed until the funeral is over, confronts bereaved people with the reality of the death in a variety of ways and with the help of many different people, from family and friends to strangers. As pastoral theologian Edgar Jackson wrote, a funeral serves "healthful ends when it is conducted in an atmosphere that permits facing reality not only personally but socially. When a number of other people accept a fact, it is increasingly difficult for one or two members of the group to deny it" (1963, 38). Paul Irion identified this view as the psychosocial perspective on funerals in his excellent book *The Funeral: Vestige or Value?* (1966, 90–97). Likewise Beverley Raphael, in *The Anatomy of Bereavement,* emphasized how the public nature of funerals helps the bereaved accept the reality of the death (1983, 37–39).

A psychosocial perspective by itself, however, is inadequate for understanding funerals, because there are a variety of ways the bereaved could come together for public mourning other than funerals. A hall and a band could be rented for a dinner, or a home opened to those invited. Why do human beings prefer funerals and memorial services? There must be more to the story, which brings us to the funeral seen as a rite of passage.

The Funeral as a Rite of Passage

Like all funerals, a Christian funeral is what the French cultural anthropologist Arnold van Gennep called a rite of passage in his book *The Rites of Passage.* Though the original French version was published in 1908 (according to the English translators), it was not until an English translation appeared in 1960 that Van Gennep's understanding of funerals and other rites of passage, such as weddings, began influencing the English-speaking world. For instance, Paul Irion wrote about Van Gennep's model in *The Funeral: Vestige or Value?* (1966, 90–97). In the late 1960s, well-known cultural anthropologist Victor Turner drew on the rites-of-passage model, even using Van Gennep's liminal terminology for his own work on liminality and *communitas* (Turner, 1969, 94–97). Increasingly, the phrase "rite of passage" is becoming incorporated into the language of contemporary culture and finding its way into academic works (for instance, see Willimon, 1979, 101–6; Raphael, 1983, 37–39; Sullender, 1985, 144–67; Ramshaw, 1987, 42–45; and Noren, 2001, 96).

According to Van Gennep, rites of passage have to do with "all the ceremonial patterns which accompany a passage from one situation to another or from one cosmic or social world to another" (1960, 10). There are many such rites, but some of the main ones he wrote about are rites of pregnancy and childbirth, initiation, betrothal and marriage, and, of course, funerals. As religion scholar Catherine Bell puts it, "rites of passage are ceremonies that accompany and dramatize such major events as birth, coming-of-age initiations for boys and girls, marriage, and death. Sometimes called 'life-crisis' or 'life-cycle' rites, they culturally mark a person's transition from one stage of social life to another" (1997, 94).

Van Gennep subdivided the rites of passage into three parts, which he named rites of separation, transition rites, and rites of incorporation. He also called them preliminal, liminal, and postliminal rites (1960, 11). According to Victor Turner, liminal has a Latin root meaning "threshold" (1969, 94). Catherine Bell says that these three subdivisions are stages through which a person passes in a rite of passage. The separation stage focuses on "the person's removal from one social grouping" (1997, 36). The transition stage dramatizes the change going on "by holding the person in a 'betwixt and between' state for a period of time" (36). And, the incorporation stage "reincorporates him or her into a new identity and status within another social grouping" (36).

Any one of the three stages may be emphasized, depending on the particular situation. For instance, Van Gennep wrote, "rites of separation are prominent in funeral ceremonies, rites of incorporation at marriages" (11). However, he also was quick to point out that just because one subdivision may appear more prominent in a particular situation, the other two also are present and may play a more significant role in the rite of passage than at first imagined. This is as true for funerals as it is for other life crisis rites. Indeed, Van Gennep began his chapter on funerals by making this point:

> On first considering funeral ceremonies, one expects rites of separation to be their most prominent component, in contrast to rites of transition and rites of incorporation, which should be only slightly elaborated. A study of the data, however, reveals that the rites of separation are few in number and very simple, while the transition rites have a duration and complexity sometimes so great that they must be granted a sort of autonomy.

Furthermore, those funeral rites which incorporate the deceased into the world of the dead are most extensively elaborated and assigned the greatest importance. (146)

In the manner of cultural anthropologists writing in the early twentieth century, Van Gennep illustrated his model using numerous cases of tribal cultures and religions from around the world, along with ancient texts describing funeral practices from long ago, most of which would seem utterly foreign to contemporary Western people. Yet, his discussion does include some description that seems relevant to contemporary Western culture, and in some instances he does focus on Christianity. So the brief discussion below of the three stages focuses only on a tiny portion of what is a vast, complex situation when funerals from around the world, and from history, are considered.

The Separation Stage in Funerals

Van Gennep listed numerous rites of separation associated with funerals, many of which seem strange to contemporary people. Some of these include such things as procedures for transporting the corpse outside, burning the possessions of the deceased, rites of purification, and various taboos. Another kind of separation involves destruction of the corpse, which has been done in different ways for different purposes. The one most familiar to contemporary people is cremation. Another type of separation rite occurs when the corpse is buried rather than destroyed. It involves physical procedures of separation such as with a coffin and a grave, or other less familiar things. "The closing of the coffin or the tomb is often a particularly solemn conclusion to the entire ceremony" (1960, 164).

Notice how the emphasis is on the literal, physical process of separating the living from the dead. If we begin at the point of death, this is indeed the emphasis today. The body is taken from the home, the hospital room, the scene of the accident, or from wherever the death occurred. This initial separation of the body from the newly bereaved marks the beginning of funeral preparation, or memorial service preparation, as the corpse ultimately ends up at the funeral home or crematorium.

When the separation is seen as the first of the three stages constituting a rite of passage, this initial separation of the body from the bereaved in preparation for the funeral gives way to the second stage, transition. However, there are additional times of separation during the whole funeral process, which makes separation and the other two stages seem more like three perspectives on funerals than a sequence of stages. Thus, a second time of separation takes place during the transition stage, when the family members, having viewed the body for the last time, see the casket closed. If the funeral is in the funeral home, this final closing may occur at the end of the funeral service, but if the funeral is in the church, it normally occurs right before the service. Finally, the third time of separation is at the cemetery, when the casket, or urn, is buried.

When the living and the dead are being separated, the mourners are separating themselves from more than a body. They are separating themselves from a relationship with the deceased, when the deceased was still alive, and from a complex of relationships that included the deceased. The various groups that included the deceased will have to reconfigure themselves. Finally, just as the incorporation stage marks the end of the suspension from daily life in society, so the separation stage marks the beginning of the suspension for the mourners so that they can take the time they need for going through the funeral rite of passage.

The Transition Stage in Funerals

Van Gennep spent much of his time on transition rites, and he found that these funeral rites could be extensive. The transition stage occurs between the initial separation from the corpse and the incorporation stage that marks the end of the transition period. For us, this means that the days spent preparing for the funeral, attending the visitation, and participating in the funeral service constitute the time in which mourners are in the "betwixt and between" state, as Bell described it above. From this standpoint, it becomes possible to see how various rites of separation, such as closing the casket either before or after the funeral service, can help mourners envision an end to the transition stage. The transition stage will be discussed more extensively later in the context of mourning.

The Incorporation Stage in Funerals

The incorporation stage in the funeral rite of passage marks the end of the transition. Van Gennep mentioned, as one example, a shared meal following the funeral service. The purpose of this meal, and of the incorporation stage, is "to reunite all the surviving members of the group with each other, and sometimes also with the deceased, in the same way that a chain which has been broken by the disappearance of one of its links must be rejoined" (1960, 164–65).

In my own pastoral experience, I have found meals following the burial to be a meaningful ending to the funeral. Much energy has been spent, and sitting down to a meal provides an opportunity for the mourners to be nourished and renewed, to relax a bit, and to see that they made it through what may have been for some the most difficult day of their lives. Now, the mourners have a new bond with one another, they are veterans of the funeral, something they will share for the rest of their lives and that has become the latest chapter in the bereaved family's collective history. Leaving after this meal returns the mourners to daily life, post-funeral. There are flights home, a return to work or school, and most importantly, the challenge of facing daily life without the deceased, as the next grieving and mourning challenges await them.

Mourning in the Funeral Rite of Passage

One result of immersing himself in the study of funerals was that Van Gennep's understanding of mourning changed. Before writing his book on the rites of passage, he saw mourning as practices marking a time of isolation from society:

> Mourning, which I formerly saw simply as an aggregate of taboos and negative practices marking an isolation from society of those whom death, in its physical reality, had placed in a sacred, impure state, now appears to me to be a more complex phenomenon. (1960, 146–47)

His new understanding of mourning was tied up intimately with the three stages in the funeral rite of passage: "It is a transitional period for the survivors, and they enter it through rites of separation and emerge from it through rites of reintegration into society (rites of the lifting of mourning)" (147).

This view of mourning places some strain on the word transition, at least in the English translation of Van Gennep's book, because transition has to do double duty. When the focus is on funeral rites, it refers to the second stage of the funeral rite of passage. But when the focus is on the survivors, it refers to their experience during this time. Mourning is a "transitional period" for them, which is marked by the three stages constituting the funeral rite of passage. Thank goodness the translators of the original French version of Van Gennep's book did not translate the French word for "passage" as *transition,* as they could have done.

Viewing mourning as a transition is far more fruitful than seeing it as isolation, because it opens up insight into another essential feature of mourning that cannot be seen so easily through the lens of isolation. Van Gennep observed: "In some cases, the transitional period of the living is a counterpart of the transitional period of the deceased, and the termination of the first sometimes coincides with the termination of the second—that is, with the incorporation of the deceased into the world of the dead" (1960, 147). As a result of this observation about mourning, Van Gennep also could say that during mourning the survivors and the deceased form a "special group, situated between the world of the living and the world of the dead" (147). During this mourning time, "social life is suspended for all those affected by it, and the length of the period increases with the closeness of social ties to the deceased (e.g., for widows, relatives), and with a higher social standing of the dead person" (148).

This correspondence between the journey of the dead to their new home and the mourning of the bereaved is maintained throughout Van Gennep's discussion of the three stages in the funeral rite of passage. The funeral is both for the living and the dead. The deceased person made a separation from the living through death, but the survivors need a rite for beginning their separation. In the transition stage, mourning corresponds to the journey the deceased is making to a final home. Indeed, the most significant reason for making the mourning transition is to assist the deceased on the journey. The transition stage is composed of rites that enable the mourners and the deceased to fulfill this purpose. For instance, among his many examples, Van Gennep tells about a people called the Lapps, who made sure to kill a reindeer on the grave so that the deceased could ride it to the final destination, which was a difficult journey lasting at least three weeks or, some have said, three years (1960, 154).

Although the notion of an extended journey being necessary for the deceased may sound strange to our ears, it has been conceived in numerous ways in human history, ways that take many different amounts of time. So some mourning transitions correspond to funeral preparation and a ceremony taking a very brief period, whereas others may involve a series of rites extending over months or even years in some cases. Whether mourning proceeds by painting the face of the dead body or by picking out clothes that the dead body will wear during the visitation, the transition is coordinated with the funeral and with the way that religion and culture view the deceased.

Finally, the end of the mourning transition also corresponds to the end of the journey. Incorporation rites mark the end of the journey in which the deceased is incorporated into the home of the dead. If, for instance, the home of the dead is the grave, the ceremony at the cemetery can be seen as a rite of incorporation, whereas tossing dirt on the casket or placing a flower on it before it is buried can be seen as rites of separation for the mourners, within the context of incorporation for the deceased. Rites of incorporation also mark the end of the transition for the bereaved, who now have completed their task of helping the deceased and are free to return to daily life in society, only with the changes that life brings without the deceased.

Mourning, then, is what the mourners, the survivors, go through by participating in the funeral rite of passage for the purpose of helping the deceased arrive at a final, eternal destination, the home of the dead, however that may be conceived. Simultaneously, mourning is a transition helping the mourners take a temporary leave of absence from daily responsibilities and then return to daily living in the community while learning to live without the deceased, having done their duty to their dead loved one.

It is evident that a temporary suspension from routine daily life followed by an end to the suspension is very important for the mourners, because they return to daily life without the deceased. However, the mere fact of being reincorporated into society pales in significance to the more profound goal of facilitating the journey of the deceased loved one into a final home. In this respect, every funeral is religious at heart, because it has to do with the eternal destination of the deceased. It should be no surprise, then, that a Christian funeral is based on Easter, as the liturgical books have said.

Funerals, Mourning, and the Grief Process

When we add the psychological understanding of grief, with its corresponding view of mourning, to the mix of mourning and the funeral rite of passage, startling things happen. It is like adding a chemical to a formula that was stable, but the new chemical destabilizes the formula, causing it to become volatile. Notice that Van Gennep focused on mourners and mourning seen in relation to the deceased, funerals, and society. In the psychological understanding of grief, however, mourning is related only to the subjective reactions of the bereaved individual going through the grief process. Mourning, seen in relation to grief, has been disconnected from funeral rites and from society, even society at the level of the family and local community. No wonder psychotherapists have been called our secular priests!

In addition, Van Gennep carefully allowed for many differences between cultures and traditions: "What I have said holds in general, but the same act does not have the same consequences among all peoples, and I want to reiterate that I do not claim an absolute universality or an absolute necessity for the pattern of rites of passage" (1960, 161). In the psychological understanding of grief, however, neither cultural differences among mourners nor sensitivity to different consequences of mourning among different peoples is on the radar screen.

These two different views of mourning present ministers who officiate at funerals with a dilemma in pastoral care of the bereaved. If they understand mourning as a transition associated with the funeral rite of passage, they are left without an understanding of how mourning is related to grief. But if ministers understand mourning only in association with the psychological understanding of grief, they are left without an understanding of how mourning is related to funerals. In either case, relating funerals to pastoral care becomes very difficult, because the relationship among funerals, mourning, and grief remains unexplained.

The Bridge of Mourning

Traditionally, psychiatrists and psychologists have drawn a deep line in the sand between mourning associated with funeral rites and mourning associated with the grief of the individual. This is in accord with traditional divisions between academic disciplines and related professions that generate differing approaches to research and writing. In *The Anatomy of Bereavement,* Beverley Raphael reflects this division when she begins discussing mourning: "Mourning will be used here to refer to the psychological mourning processes that occur in bereavement...The rituals of mourning, such as burial, are discussed separately" (1983, 33). Even though the bereaved are helped to face the reality of the death through funerals, this entire process is seen most typically as preparation for psychological mourning that really gets under way after the funeral. Therese Rando also follows the traditional division between mourning associated with funeral rites and mourning associated with the grief process (see 1993, 23). Nevertheless, her understanding of grief and mourning is helpful for showing how funerals, mourning, and grief are related.

As we have seen, in Rando's work the first phase of grief, the avoidance phase, is coordinated explicitly with the first R process, recognizing the loss through acknowledging the death and understanding it. Recognizing the loss is the part of the psychological understanding of mourning that performs the function of helping the bereaved person move through the avoidance phase of grief. What is not generally acknowledged, however, is that this part of mourning, recognizing the loss, plays out by means of the funeral rite of passage, or at the very least in the funeral context, including its separation, transition, and incorporation stages. From the point of the death, the bereaved prepare for the funeral, attend the visitation and go to the funeral service, all of which provide the main way that the bereaved mourn at this time.

Avoidance

Mourning is the bridge connecting funerals and the avoidance phase of grief. Go in one direction across the bridge, and you come upon funeral rites. Go in the other direction, and you come upon shock and denial. The bridge of mourning helps the bereaved experience the connection between funeral rites and their grief. At my grandfather's burial, mentioned earlier, my mourning showed how mourning relates the funeral rite with the first phase of grief. On the one hand, my attempt to recognize the loss of my grandfather went hand in hand with the incorporation stage of the funeral, as I stood near the grave and talked to family members. Though my family did not plan to stay at the cemetery for so long, that time became an impromptu rite of incorporation, which perhaps is experienced more commonly through a meal following the burial. On the other hand, in the midst of this rite, my denial was being challenged as I struggled to envision my grandfather in a state of death.

With mourning as the bridge, it becomes possible to look more closely at the relationship between funerals and grief. Going back and forth across the bridge indicates that grief is not collapsed into the funeral, but that there is interaction between the two, which is helpful to those going through the mourning. This interaction can be seen in the three stages of the funeral rite of passage.

Separation

Mourning is the bridge connecting funerals and grief in the separation stage of the funeral rite of passage. Walk across the bridge to the separation stage, which signals the separation of the living from the dead. Mourners are beginning to separate from the dead body, from a relationship that existed while the deceased person was still alive, and from daily life in society necessary for having the time to go through the funeral rite of passage. Now, as you are being impacted by the funeral, walk in the other direction to the avoidance phase of grief. Mourners are attempting to recognize the loss as they prepare for the funeral, attend the visitation, and participate in the funeral service. This recognition initiates separation that will be a long process known as undoing psychosocial ties to the deceased. Without the social time-out that funeral preparation and participation bring, it would be harder for the bereaved to find time for mourning psychologically in the initial phase of grief.

Transition

Mourning is the bridge connecting funerals and grief in the transition stage of the funeral rite of passage. Once more, walk across the bridge to the funeral, this time in the transition stage where you encounter a focus on the deceased. Van Gennep made clear that the mourners and the deceased form a "special group" during the funeral rite of passage, as the mourners help the deceased make the journey to the home of the dead by participating in the rites making up the second stage of the funeral rite of passage. Now, walk across to the other side, the avoidance phase of grief. Therese Rando has made clear that the bereaved focus on the deceased during mourning in the avoidance phase of grief. Recognizing the loss through acknowledging the death and attempting to understand what caused it require such a focus.

Beyond the most practical part of the need to acknowledge the death and understand its cause, additional concerns about the deceased may be going on in the minds of bereaved individuals. Merely recognizing the loss does not take adequate account of concern about the eternal fate of the deceased, concern about the deceased receiving justice and concern about the relationship between God and the deceased. Finally, the desire to honor the deceased through memorializing requires a focus on the dead person.

As we saw earlier in this chapter, neither acknowledging the death nor understanding its cause escape the context of the funeral preparation and ceremony. As mourners walk back and forth across the bridge, they bring with them the impact of each encounter with the funeral and with their grief, so that the funeral influences the way they experience their grief, and their grief influences their experience of the funeral.

Incorporation

Mourning is the bridge connecting funerals and grief in the incorporation stage of the funeral rite of passage. One final time, walk across the bridge to the funeral. In the incorporation stage, you encounter the ending of the transition, completion of the process, anticipation of returning to daily life. The counterpart to this is that the deceased is being incorporated into the home of the dead, whether it is the grave or heaven. Van Gennep's image of surviving group members reuniting, quoted earlier, is apt. Incorporation rites "reunite all the surviving members of the group with each other, and sometimes also with the deceased, in the same way that a chain which has been broken by the disappearance of one of its links must be rejoined" (1960, 164–65).

Reverse course, and walk back across the bridge to grief. It has been several days or perhaps as much as a week since the death occurred, and now the funeral is at an end. Shock has worn off, and denial has been challenged. You are making some progress in acknowledging the reality of the death, and you have some understanding of its cause and the circumstances in which it happened. It may have taken several days to get the story of what happened, but now you have heard it. There have been tears and laughter, and you have reconnected with relatives and with some family friends you have not seen for years. Your mind begins returning to practical details. You have to catch the early flight tomorrow morning and need someone to drive you to the airport.

The incorporation stage of the funeral interacts with the avoidance phase of grief as the mourners move toward completion of this phase to whatever degree possible. When the loss is recognized to some significant extent, the next phase of grief appears on the horizon and will become increasingly prominent as the funeral becomes a memory. Yet, ending the transition and being reincorporated into daily life in society is not all that mourning involves during the incorporation stage. Just as there is a focus on the deceased in the transition stage, there is a related focus in the incorporation stage. Continuing with Van Gennep's terminology, this focus is on the deceased being incorporated into the home of the dead.

Although this terminology is foreign to us, it does serve to highlight part of our experience metaphorically. In Christian funerals, we commend the deceased to God, and we carefully place the body in what will be its "final resting place." You would think that this is where funerals and grief part company, but this is not true. Although the language is different, recognizing the reality of the death does not mean that the bereaved person no longer relates to the deceased. Rather, in the psychological understanding of grief, the new home of the dead is in the memory of the grieving person. As Anderson and Foley point out, "When death occurs, one kind of relationship with the deceased ends and another begins. Effecting the transition from relating to a living presence to building an enduring memory is the work of grieving" (1998, 113).

Historically, look at the way psychiatrist Erich Lindemann described the relationship between the bereaved and the deceased in his work with hospitalized victims of the famous Coconut Grove fire in Boston. He wrote that patients who accepted their need to go through the grief process "embarked on a program of dealing in memory with the deceased person" (1979, 65). This required the bereaved to review their relationship with the deceased over time and to become acquainted with their own changing emotional reactions to the deceased. (The psychological understanding of this review process ultimately is rooted in the view of Sigmund Freud set forth in "Mourning and Melancholia" and is helpfully described by Beverley Raphael in some detail [1983, 44–45].) When the bereaved reached a certain point of accepting the death, it did not mean that the relationship with the deceased was ended. Rather, according to Lindemann, the bereaved had to work out the way they were going to relate to the deceased in the future. In memory, there was an ongoing "future relationship to the deceased" (1979, 75).

It seems that psychiatry, by developing the psychological understanding of grief, has envisioned a new home for the dead in the memory of the bereaved. Although the memory will develop over time, as the bereaved person experiences the grief process, this new memory is being born in rudimentary form even as newly bereaved people are trying to recognize the loss and are participating in the funeral rite of passage. This is why mourning continues acting as a bridge between the funeral and grief during the incorporation stage.

Mourning and Memory

The funeral is over, and the mourners are back home. The bridging function of mourning is ended, right? Well, not quite. Something traditionally ignored in the psychological understanding of grief is that the funeral is included in the memory of the bereaved, because the funeral contains the last memory of the dead person in which the body was still present, or when the ashes were new. If the funeral is religious, the deceased was seen in relation to the divine. Many details, and much content, of the funeral may be forgotten, but the funeral becomes as much a part of memory associated with the deceased as anything else.

It may be that mourning continues acting as a bridge between the funeral and grief, in memory, throughout the grief process. It may be that just as human beings can revisit other important events from the past and learn valuable lessons from them, so they can revisit the funeral and pick its fruit that was not ready to be eaten until time had passed. This may include remembering bare facts or renewed relationships, a song sung or a sentence spoken, a prayer said or a scripture passage read, a positive and meaningful experience or something that seemed negative. The nourishment we gain from the fruit of our past certainly does not come only from positive experiences, and this includes negative funeral experiences.

It also may be that, among church members, mourning continues performing its bridging function between the church and grief throughout the grief process. See chapter 11 for more discussion of this.

Finally, the funeral not only is part of memory in the grief process of individuals. It also becomes part of a family history that may be brought up again and again over time. In some instances, it even becomes part of the collective memory of a church, community, or society.

Differences between Funeral Stages and the Grief Process

Van Gennep subdivided the funeral rite of passage into three stages, including separation, transition, and incorporation. Mourning as transition begins with separation and ends with incorporation. Rando divides the grief process into three phases, or stages, including the avoidance phase, which has been discussed; the confrontation phase; and the accommodation phase. In the confrontation phase, one of the several mourning processes during this time involves the kind of emotional review discussed earlier in the discussion about the relationship between the bereaved and the deceased. Accommodation marks the end of the grief process, when the bereaved person can live fruitfully in the world again. In this phase, mourning is geared toward reinvesting in the world. In the funeral, and in the grief process, mourning is what enables the bereaved to move through the three stages to completion.

One major difference between the rite of passage stages and the grief process phases is the length of time it takes to move through all three stages in each one. If the funeral is seen as being completed within a few days of the death, it contrasts greatly with the grief process taking months and years. However, as Van Gennep pointed out, funerals throughout the world and in history have taken innumerably different amounts of time. Similarly, grief is envisioned as having an ending, which is completion of the third phase. Because of the need for an ending to the third phase, there have been attempts to name the length of time it takes to finish grieving, but usually this is too short.

Conclusion

Funerals, mourning, and grief are related in meaningful ways. Consequently, this relationship has an important implication for pastoral care of the bereaved. It is that the funeral rite (or rites) of passage provides the primary means of caring for the bereaved during the first phase of grief, because caring in this instance involves facilitating the very mourning that occurs through funerals. Finally, this understanding of pastoral care contains an additional implication for ministers who officiate at funerals, which will be discussed in the next chapter.

CHAPTER NINE

Worship Leadership in Funerals

You may think that I am placing a heavy burden on you by suggesting in the last chapter that pastoral care seen in relation to the funeral involves facilitating mourning. This may sound like something that might be said about a pastoral counseling relationship, in which a pastoral counselor is working with a bereaved individual, but this is not what I mean. Instead, what I mean by facilitating mourning is simply that you help bring about mourning occurring in relation to a funeral by means of your worship leadership in the funeral. Your worship leadership helps bring about mourning by enabling the mourners to participate in the funeral liturgy. Nor is your ministry occurring before the funeral left out of this. Your personal interactions with the bereaved before the funeral, your participation in the visitation, and your funeral planning culminate in your funeral worship leadership.

Still, the phrase "pastoral care" automatically may make you think of your relationship to a particular bereaved person, so that the funeral now becomes like a therapeutic technique you are using as a means of caring for the bereaved person. In this view, what you say in the funeral corresponds analogically to therapeutic responses made to a church member or client in private pastoral care or counseling conversation. Now, every word or sentence you utter becomes the important thing that will either evoke grief or will hinder it. This is the real guilt-producing burden some ministers have carried.

If you cannot get out of this mind-set, the connection between your pastoral care and worship leadership will always remain a foreign concept to you. However, if you will allow yourself to consider the possibility that worship leadership can be a genuine means of pastoral care, a funeral in this instance, then a different way of understanding your pastoral care emerges. In this different way, you are concerned with putting the funeral liturgy into practice as the way that you are caring for the bereaved, because you understand that it is their participation in the funeral liturgy that matters. This view of caring for the bereaved through funerals may sound positive to you, because it indicates that pastoral care occurs through what you do normally as a minister. Yet, at the same time, this view may give you a narcissistic wound, because any number of people can lead funeral worship as well as you can, and the funeral is going to happen whether or not you are the one leading it. For the mourners, funeral preparation, the visitation and participating in the funeral liturgy are the important things.

Your actual burden, then, or your responsibility, is to embark on a spiritual journey over time as you experience funerals, in order to focus on the funeral liturgy with increasing confidence and clarity, so that you can put it into practice for the sake of the mourners. In this chapter, I will discuss three themes encountered on this journey, including grief, death, and hope.

Encountering Grief

The first essential theme to encounter on your spiritual journey is grief. As well as you are able, you should accept the reality that mourners bring the pain of their grief to funerals, including shock, denial, and the psychological, behavioral, social, and physical reactions comprising the first phase of grief. Sometimes shock will have worn off, but not always. And some may experience far stronger denial than others, to the point where they feel hardly anything throughout the funeral, whereas others may have eruptions of emotion. Overall, it is a safe bet that differing degrees of denial combined with differing degrees of emotion will be present among the mourners.

As you can see, accepting the presence of grief in a funeral includes openness to mourners having different experiences in the funeral. There is no one correct response, because not every mourner will have the same mixture of shock; denial; and psychological, behavioral, social, and physical reactions. Moreover, different mourners will have had different kinds of relationships with the deceased. For this reason, you can take yourself off the hook of thinking that mourners must respond in certain ways or you are doing a bad job. Just let the first phase of grief in all its variety be a natural part of the mix in the funeral, so that you are not saddled with avoidance of grief in your worship leadership.

If you must avoid grief, your own or that of the mourners, you may worry excessively about which biblical passages to read, or struggle unnecessarily with saying just the right thing in your prayers. Your whole approach to the funeral may be an expression of fear that some part of the liturgy will take the mourners, or yourself, in the direction of experiencing the pain of grief. Ironically, because denial is such an important part of the grief process at this point, you have far less control over what mourners experience subjectively than you might imagine, and there may be a far greater variety of subjective reactions in the funeral than you can know. For instance, a mourner who also is grieving a previous loss may be experiencing thoughts and feelings about that loss, while hardly being able to focus on the present funeral.

One of the great caring gifts you can give every mourner is your willingness to say what needs to be said, whether it is something as simple as "We are going to miss Joe," or whether it is something as profound as "None of us can escape death." If you realize that different mourners will hear you differently, and that there will be different responses, you can be more free to speak, because you never can say just the right thing to everyone, and you never can have one right response from every mourner. Indeed, you never will know what most people are thinking and feeling throughout the funeral.

Recall the burial scene at my grandfather's funeral, discussed in chapter 8. During the funeral worship, before the burial, the minister said something that I found helpful at the time and that I have always remembered, though he was a complete stranger and we never did talk privately. In one part of the sermon, he talked about how my grandmother would miss her husband, and he gave an example. He said something like this: "You'll start walking up the stairs in your house, and as you take hold of the banister, it will remind you of him grasping the banister and walking up the stairs. Perhaps you'll lovingly run your hand over the wood and linger there for a moment." This helped me in a very fundamental way. I was worried about my grandmother and how she was going to survive. Basically, I just did not know what to expect in the months to come. The image of my grandmother grieving, and yet continuing to live her life, eased my worry. It gave me some confidence that she, and all of us, would be okay.

Getting Personal

No, I don't mean you talking about yourself. Instead, I mean talking about the deceased, and to the mourners in the funeral. A funeral sermon may contain such discussion, which is much easier if the presence of grief is accepted, as it was in my grandfather's funeral. This may seem to be a matter of course today, yet as recently as the mid-twentieth century, making this point about allowing for discussion of the deceased and the bereaved seemed urgent. For instance, Paul Irion, in *The Funeral: Vestige or Value?*, reported on a survey of 160 Protestant ministers from different parts of the United States, who provided information about more than 2,000 funerals they had conducted during the previous year (1966, 14). The survey included questions about the elements making up mid-twentieth century funerals, which were parts of the liturgy, including music, scripture readings, prayers, and sermons. Out of these four parts of the funeral liturgy, prayers and sermons provide opportunities for discussing the deceased and mentioning the mourners. In prayers, for instance, nearly all the pastors surveyed "offered prayers centered around intercession for the mourners in their need and thanksgiving for the providence of God" (16). Praying for the bereaved in their grief reflects accepting the presence of grief in funerals, and it seems that the mid-twentieth century pastors did a good job with this. However, when it came to sermons, the situation was quite different.

As we saw in the previous chapter, sermons can include discussion of the deceased, and sermons can be coordinated with discussion of the deceased by others, such as family members or friends who speak briefly in the funeral. However, according to Irion, in the 1960s some clergy assumed the sermon should be omitted from the funeral liturgy, though 80 percent of the pastors surveyed reported that they did preach a brief funeral sermon, the most common themes being "efforts to meet the personal needs of the mourners, conveying the comfort of the Christian faith, and interpreting the Christian understanding of death" (Irion, 1966, 17). Yet, even though these pastors did preach funeral sermons, only about 40 percent of them ever made any personal reference to the deceased in the sermon. Fewer still used obituary material for factual statements about family relationships the deceased maintained in life, and only a handful used a eulogy (17).

Later in the book, Irion commented on these survey results: "In other words, it is quite possible that many funeral services literally make no mention of the person who has died nor of the relationships that have been sustained with the deceased" (50). Then he went on to express his concern:

> Some of this objectivity is due to a perfectly legitimate desire to avoid the pitfalls of lavish eulogies, but all too often it represents an effort to minimize the painful personal involvement of the mourner in recalling his past experience with the deceased, thus circumventing his encounter with the reality of death. (50)

One contemporary Presbyterian minister who went to seminary in the 1960s has written about his effort to escape this trap, showing how such changes often are generational struggles. In the introduction of his article, "To Preach or Not to Preach: That is the (Funeral) Question," James Lowry begins autobiographically: "In the mid 1960s when I graduated from seminary, the prevailing wisdom among Presbyterian clergy in general and teachers of Presbyterian worship in particular was that there be no preaching at funerals" (1999, 39). Later in the paragraph, he explains why sermons were to be omitted: "Sermons or even brief meditations were to be avoided lest the preacher be tempted, on the one hand, to lapse into a eulogy where the focus would be on the deceased rather than on God; or, on the other hand, be tempted to use the occasion to bring the lost and errant among the bereaved into the fold" (39).

Though sermons were to be omitted, other parts of the funeral liturgy were acceptable:

> Funeral services, we were taught, were always to have readings from the Old Testament, readings from the New Testament, and a pastoral prayer. In addition, hymns might be sung and the Apostles' Creed "recited." The passages of scripture to be read should be chosen carefully to suit the occasion, and the pastoral prayer, in addition to petitions on behalf of the bereaved, should include mention of gratitude for particular attributes of the deceased as well as contributions he or she had made to the church or community. (Lowry, 1999, 39)

Casting off what he had been taught about sermons was a slow process: "In my ministry, that wisdom went unquestioned for more than a decade. Since that time, however, I have come to a growing conclusion that preaching at funerals is an important act of ministry for those willing to commit the time and energy to do it with theological integrity" (Lowry, 1999, 39).

In the present time, rubrics in liturgical books clearly provide space for discussing the deceased in Christian funerals, and they do not shy away from sermons in this regard. As the worship leader, the more you can accept your own grief and that of the mourners, the more effectively you can speak about the deceased, and to the mourners, in the funeral.

Encountering Death

The second theme on your spiritual journey is death itself. In a Christian funeral, the liturgy does not avoid the reality of death, but provides ample opportunity for acknowledging it through scripture readings, prayers, lyrics of songs, and sermons. For instance, one of the classic scripture passages read in funerals is Isaiah 40:1–11. Consider verses 6–8:

> A voice says, "Cry out!"
>   And I said, "What shall I cry?"
> All people are grass,
>   their constancy is like the flower of the field.
> The grass withers, the flower fades,
>   when the breath of the LORD blows upon it;
>   surely the people are grass.
> The grass withers, the flower fades;
>   but the word of our God will stand forever.

A human life withers like the grass, and fades like the flower, until it is gone. In the casket, or in the urn, lie the remains of one whose life has gone.

If you find yourself consistently avoiding scripture passages that either mention death directly or allude to death, you may be avoiding the reality of death out of fear. You may fear that the mourners will be upset or angry at hearing it and being confronted with death, or you may be avoiding it yourself, or both. This is a spiritual issue with which you are called to wrestle if you are a worship leader in funerals. It is not easy to stand in the presence of death, much less to talk about it appropriately in the most emotionally delicate of situations. Yet, here you are, the one who gives voice to the reality of death in the funeral.

There is some good news about this, however. Your job is not to reinvent the wheel by coming up with novel things to say in the funeral. Instead, your creativity and style of worship leadership are placed in the service of putting the funeral liturgy into play. You do not have to improve on the words of Isaiah, Paul, or Jesus; you just have to put them before the congregation. You do not change the words of scripture; you read them. The same is true of funeral hymns. You sing the lyrics; you do not rewrite them. By the same token, however, prayer and sermons do require your own words, which means that you will have to say some things about death in your own words.

Liturgical books can be helpful here, especially with regard to prayers. You can use funeral prayers found in the service books, sometimes revising them to fit the situation, or reflecting on them as jumping off points for creating your own prayers. For example, consider one prayer found in the Presbyterian service book, the *Book of Common Worship*. The first half of this prayer draws on Isaiah 40:6–8, part of the passage quoted above:

> Eternal God, we acknowledge the uncertainty of our life on earth.
> We are given a mere handful of days, and our span of life seems
>   nothing in your sight.
> All flesh is as grass; and all its beauty is like the flower of the field.
> The grass withers, the flower fades; but your word will stand
>   forever. (917)

It is possible for you to draw on this prayer word for word, but you may revise it to fit the situation. Or as you reflect on it during your funeral preparation, it may inspire you to draw on an entirely different scripture passage for your first prayer. This different passage may speak to death as directly and poetically as the Isaiah passage, and it helps give you words for your prayer.

There is more good news. As we will see more fully in the next section on hope, death in the funeral liturgy is placed in the context of hope. Isaiah contrasts withering grass and the fading flower with the unending life of God; and the prayer quoted above expresses hope based on this contrast in its very next sentence: "In this is our hope, for you are our God" (917). The truth of death is seen in relation to the divine in Christianity. Accepting the presence of death as the worship leader means that you find the courage to read, speak, and sing about death when this is part of the liturgy. But, at the same time, you do not omit the relation of death to God in the liturgy.

One more piece of good news is that accepting the presence of death is compatible with celebrating the life of the dead person in the memorializing aspects of the funeral, discussed in the previous section on encountering grief. Family members may say that they want to celebrate the life of their dead loved one in the funeral, but they do not want to focus on the drawn-out illness, the suffering, or the horrible accident. Nor do they want to bring up the bad temper or the faults of their dead loved one. But this does not have to be seen merely as avoidance of what the dead person really was like. Rather, in part it means that there was much more to the person's life and relationships than you ever could have known.

On occasion, a family member who speaks at a funeral may be a young adult who was the grandchild, niece, or nephew of the deceased. As the pastor, you may have known the one who died only for a few years, but the young family member knew this person since infancy. A touching and loving story is told: "When I was in grade school, my grandmother made cookies for me and my brother every Saturday."

Could this be the same person who was your sparring partner on the finance committee? Acknowledging the reality of a person's death also means acknowledging the reality of their life, including the limits of our knowing that life in its fullness and in its historical richness. Remembering and celebrating the life of the dead person goes hand in hand with the recognition of their death.

This seemingly paradoxical connection also is rooted in the human being's inherent fear of death. The deceased person becomes like the hero who has faced death, as discussed by Ernest Becker in *The Denial of Death*. According to Becker,

> We admire most the courage to face death; we give such valor our highest and most constant adoration; it moves us deeply in our hearts because we have doubts about how brave we ourselves would be...And so the hero has been the center of human honor and acclaim since probably the beginning of specifically human evolution. (1973, 11–12)

The deceased person is the hero who has faced death, showing those left behind that it can be done courageously. The life of this person is celebrated, as a hero is celebrated.

When we move from a focus on the dead person whose funeral we are having to the existential fear of death that is part of the human condition, we are only a small step away from finitude itself. We stand before the reality that all human life, and indeed all existence, dies. At this point, we all stand together as one. It is at this fundamental level that Christianity speaks of hope most profoundly.

The loss of someone through death is final. The finality and eerie sense of absence forces finitude upon us, and we know it is our lot as created beings. A sense of its presence puts us in a kind of philosophical mood, as if we were together pondering the nature of things. This may not be consciously thought about, but it is a mood that can enter a funeral as if lingering in the background. This is when explicit theological statements seem to make the most sense. They boldly articulate the reality of death, not just one person's death, but the fact of death as a fundamental truth about life. And they boldly articulate God's defeat of death and divine love that will never let us go. If there is any real solidarity among human beings, surely it is in those sorts of moments, transcendent moments, when we catch a glimpse of finitude and eternity. Standing before these things is one of the most purely human and purely divine manifestations of life in human existence.

Encountering Hope

An eleven-year-old girl approached the minister after church one Sunday and asked him the following question, saying, "My dad is in heaven with God now, right?"

Three months earlier, the minister had officiated at the funeral of her father, and he knew well the context of bereavement out of which this question arose. The girl was seeking some reassurance after time had elapsed following the funeral.

His answer was a very straightforward, "Yes, he is." This seemed to satisfy the girl, who then went on her way.

Imagine that you were the minister, and it was you who said, "Yes, he is." In the privacy of your own heart, how would you have understood this response? You may have been perfectly comfortable with it, because you believe in a literal resurrection. You may have felt guilty about lying, because you reject a literal understanding of the resurrection. Or you may have said to yourself that you were not lying, because your view of the resurrection is that "something happened," though you are confused about how to understand it. Speaking of stumbling blocks, the resurrection is something with which you must come to grips, in one way or another, if you are to officiate at funerals, because Christian funeral worship is built upon the resurrection, the great Christian symbol of hope.

According to the dictionary, hope involves desire combined with expectation (see Capps, 1995, and Lester, 1995, for helpful discussions of hope). In Christianity, hope is based on the New Testament writings about the resurrection of Jesus. So, simply put, Christian hope can be characterized as the desire for eternal life with God combined with the expectation of attaining this new life following death. There are several related issues that make dealing with Christian hope particularly challenging. One is how you interpret the New Testament writings on the resurrection, especially whether you interpret it literally or nonliterally. Another interpretive issue involves how you see resurrection in relation to present-day Christian people. If Christians say that they believe in the resurrection, what exactly do you understand them to be saying? On the one hand, dying and rising can be understood metaphorically as perhaps the most fundamental dynamic within human life, so that it is not meant to address eternal life literally (see Stairs, 2000, 73–106). It certainly cannot be denied that many Christian people do not have a literalistic view of the resurrection. On the other hand, many Christian people do believe in a literal resurrection and correspondingly do hope for a literal eternal life with God on the other side of death, though this can be expressed in enormously different ways with the help of different theologies.

The third interpretive issue relates directly to the funeral. In bereavement situations, the issue is not the death of a job or the death of a marriage. It is the literal death of a person. It would seem that one criterion for an adequate interpretation of the resurrection is that it address the literal death of a person in a meaningful way. An important consideration in this regard is that the hope of the survivors becomes connected to their hope for the deceased, and their hope for the deceased may include the strong need for justice. The vision of eternity involves a quality of life that more than makes up for all the undeserved, unfair, and senseless suffering the deceased person endured in this life.

As a symbol, the resurrection can be seen similarly to the symbol of the cross (see Setzer, 2001, on resurrection as a symbol in ancient Judaism). Looking briefly at the cross can be helpful for understanding the resurrection symbolically. Assume there was a literal cross on which Jesus was executed. Whatever it actually looked like, it is long gone. When we talk about the cross, we are not referring to the literal material used for killing Jesus. Rather, the cross represents something beyond that literal piece of wood. It represents a host of spiritual matters involving God in relation to human beings, such as sacrifice, salvation, forgiveness, atonement, and love. When it comes to the resurrection, however, there is nothing material, like a piece of wood, to which we can point. Nevertheless, the resurrection as found in the New Testament represents a host of spiritual matters centering around God in relation to human beings and all creation. Death and life are put in an ultimate context. God is responding to death.

And why not? Why can we not consider God in relation to death? Why can we not wonder whether God is more powerful than death, and wonder about eternity? Of course, this throws us back on the question of God's nature, the concept of death, the nature of the self, Christology, and so on. This issue provides a lifetime of theological and biblical study accompanying our slowly maturing interpretation of the resurrection. Yet, here we are at the funeral, and much of our concentrated study lies ahead.

Symbols are great things, because they engage your imagination. Sometimes they can free you from laborious concern over what is literal versus what is nonliteral. As an experiment in imagination, set aside the heavy theological issues temporarily, and imagine that you accept the resurrection as true in the most childlike, naive way that you can. In your imagination, you are allowing yourself to embrace the craziest of hopes with the abandon of a child jumping into a swimming pool feet first in July. Any time you want, you can articulate a contemporary scientific understanding of death, and you can pick apart the New Testament endlessly. But for right now, you are entering the world of imagination, where you are allowed to entertain ideas and even deep desires that you do not entertain normally.

For me, the resurrection is like entering this world of imagination, where hope can be explored and embraced. In this world, having to do with ultimate things, such distinctions as literal versus nonliteral become tiresome. The imagination, far from being an escape, can be the road to understanding. Paul Tillich, in his autobiography, *On the Boundary*, wrote that when he was a young teenager, he began escaping into fantasy rather than face some difficulties he was experiencing. He went on to point out, however, that his fantasy matured into philosophical imagination that gave him a vocation (Tillich, 1966, 24–25).

Whatever your particular theological beliefs about the resurrection are, they need to be planted and taking root in the soil of your imagination, even if this begins with immature fantasy. Like it or not, you are the one who will be articulating this fundamental religious concern in the funeral, and what you believe about the resurrection on a very personal level, and consequently what you believe about hope, will influence your funeral worship leadership necessarily. This is why addressing the resurrection in the context of a spiritual journey taken over time is so important.

Resurrection in the Funeral Liturgy

Developing your understanding of the resurrection on a personal level gives you freedom to choose parts of the funeral liturgy that are about the resurrection explicitly, rather than having to avoid them. For instance, consider the initial prayer after the procession in the Episcopal funeral liturgy (*The Book of Common Prayer*, 493–94). There are several optional prayers provided, each one mentioning the resurrection. The first option says:

> O God, who by the glorious resurrection of your Son Jesus Christ destroyed death, and brought life and immortality to light: Grant that your servant *N.*, being raised with him, may know the strength of his presence, and rejoice in his eternal glory; who with you and the Holy Spirit lives and reigns, one God, for ever and ever. *Amen.*

Following the initial prayer, the worship leader is given the option of adding a second, concluding prayer that shifts the focus to comforting the bereaved. It says:

> Most merciful God, whose wisdom is beyond our understanding: Deal graciously with *NN.* in *their* grief. Surround *them* with your love, that *they* may not be overwhelmed by *their* loss, but have confidence in your goodness, and strength to meet the days to come; through Jesus Christ our Lord. *Amen.*

So far, so good. These two prayers taken together address hope and comfort while focusing on the deceased and the bereaved.

Now, let's shift to the Lutheran liturgical book and look at the first prayer in the funeral liturgy (*Lutheran Book of Worship: Ministers Desk Edition*, 332). Again, several options are given. The first prayer starts out expressing thanks for the deceased. Then, in the second half, it mentions eternal life: "Give us your aid, so we may see in death the gate to eternal life, that we may continue our course on earth in confidence until, by your call, we are reunited with those who have gone before us; through your Son, Jesus Christ our Lord. *Amen.*"

The next option, however, mentions neither resurrection nor eternal life, but focuses solely on comforting the mourners: "Almighty God, source of all mercy and giver of comfort: Deal graciously, we pray, with those who mourn, that, casting all their sorrow on you, they may know the consolation of your love; through your Son, Jesus Christ our Lord. *Amen.*"

Undoubtedly there are times when choosing this latter option is desirable. However, what if you choose it, or one like it, almost every time, and when you choose a prayer that mentions the resurrection or eternal life, it makes you feel uncomfortable? Chances are, you begin to rationalize your choice. You tell yourself that focusing on the resurrection too quickly encourages the bereaved to avoid their grief. I have heard a pastor or two talk about focusing on the resurrection in the funeral in such a way that avoiding grief seemed to be their main intent. Clearly, it is inappropriate to envision the funeral as a celebration of the resurrection as a means of avoidance. However, a genuine focus on the resurrection in a funeral does not bring about avoidance, but just the opposite. It is hard to be hopeful while being in denial of the pain that makes hope meaningful. Or, put another way, hope seen in relation to grief is not an either/or situation, but rather a both/and situation. Hope can cut through denial and free a newly bereaved person to experience grief.

Several church members and I discovered this truth one Sunday. Early on Saturday morning a church member called me and told me that her mother had died late Friday night. This was not unexpected, because her health had been declining markedly over several months. The daughter did not want a visit on Saturday, which was a busy day for me. I hardly had time to stop and reflect on the sad news. Then came the worship service on Sunday morning, in which I had the responsibility of announcing her death to the congregation and telling them that the funeral would be on the following Tuesday. To my surprise, as the choir sang their anthem during worship, the reality of her death hit me.

The choir sang the old hymn "In the Garden," which begins with these lyrics:

> I come to the garden alone, while the dew is still on the roses;
> And the voice I hear, falling on my ear, the Son of God discloses.
> And He walks with me, and He talks with me,
> And he tells me I am His own,
> And the joy we share, as we tarry there,
> None other has ever known.

I will freely confess that this particular hymn has never been a favorite of mine. But, on that Sunday morning, I heard it in a completely new way, as if for the first time. As I listened to the choir sing the first verse, I caught myself beginning to get choked up. Tears were gathering in my chest, and a few of them found escape through my eyes. I was forced to pay attention to what I was experiencing, and I quickly realized I was hearing a song about the newly deceased church member.

It was she who was walking in the garden with her Lord, but this was not the earthly garden in the New Testament, in which Mary encountered the newly risen Jesus. Now the garden was a heavenly garden, an image of eternity in which it seemed very wonderful and fitting that this church member and Jesus were walking and talking together in a beautiful place. Following the worship service, I discovered that some choir members and family members also heard the hymn this way and had grieved as well.

When the garden imagery in the hymn became a heavenly garden, any sappiness that I usually associated with the hymn disappeared. It seemed completely legitimate and appropriate. Nor did it reinforce my denial, or that of others. Rather, the heavenly image, very joyful in itself, brought out tears of grief (also see the final scene of the movie *Places in the Heart,* in which this hymn is used).

Finally, my experience of the hymn influenced my funeral preparation on Monday. I chose biblical passages presenting other heavenly images, including Isaiah 65:17–25 and Revelation 21:2, 22–25. I imagined the heavenly garden being somewhere in the new Jerusalem about which Isaiah prophesied. In Isaiah 65:18–19, the Lord says:

> But be glad and rejoice forever
>   in what I am creating;
> for I am about to create Jerusalem as a joy,
>   and its people as a delight.
> I will rejoice in Jerusalem,
>   and delight in my people;
> no more shall the sound of weeping be heard in it,
>   or the cry of distress.

I also used John's prophecy in Revelation (21:2, 22–25), which echoes Isaiah:

> And I saw the holy city, the new Jerusalem, coming down out of heaven from God, prepared as a bride adorned for her husband...I saw no temple in the city, for its temple is the Lord God the Almighty and the Lamb. And the city has no need of sun or moon to shine on it, for the glory of God is its light, and its lamp is the Lamb. The nations will walk by its light, and the kings of the earth will bring their glory into it. Its gates will never be shut by day–and there will be no night there.

Resurrection and Mourning

In a Christian funeral, the resurrection is related to mourning at each stage of the funeral rite of passage. This is another reason for coming to grips with the resurrection, in addition to being free to choose parts of the funeral liturgy that mention the resurrection or eternal life.

In the separation stage, the resurrection gently helps bereaved people begin overcoming the shock and denial that are preventing them from recognizing the death that has just occurred. The resurrection requires a focus on the dead person, including an acknowledgment that the person is no longer alive as before the death. Even though there may be a strong desire for the dead person to be alive, this desire now is being shifted to eternity. Admittedly, this shift can be used by denial in the sense that a focus on the dead person being raised to new life with God in eternity may bring temporary relief from a focus on the fact of the death. Yet, if denial can make use of the resurrection in this way, it nevertheless is a partial and temporary use that cannot overcome the recognition of death without which the notion of resurrection to eternal life makes no sense.

In the transition stage, the resurrection helps the mourners focus on the deceased, but not as mourners who can do anything to assist the deceased on the journey to the home of the dead. Notice in the first funeral prayer cited above that when the resurrection is mentioned, it involves a positive focus on the deceased being raised with Christ. In Christianity, it is not the mourners who do anything to assist the deceased on their journey, but rather it is God who raises the dead. Consequently, funeral prayers commend the deceased to God and praise God for this, rather than being requests whose fulfillment depends on something the mourners do. Praising what God is doing with regard to the deceased replaces the human effort to assist the deceased on a journey to the home of the dead.

In the incorporation stage, the resurrection presents mourners with a vision of the deceased being incorporated into an eternal home with God. In this sense, the second and third stages in a Christian funeral are closely intertwined, because there is no extended journey lasting days, weeks, or months that finally reaches an end. If the vision refers to an immediate incorporation into eternity, there is no limited time with which the mourners have to be concerned. However, if the vision is eschatological, referring to a future day of resurrection, the journey extends far beyond the lifetimes of the survivors and incorporation extends into a distant future. Theologian Jürgen Moltmann discusses this in his book, *The Coming of God: Christian Eschatology*:

> For Paul, this community with Christ, the subject of hope, extends to the dead as well as to the living. "For to this end Christ died and lived again, that he might be Lord both of the dead and of the living" (Rom. 14.9). I understand this in the following sense: In dying, Christ became the brother of the dying. In death, he became the brother of the dead. In his resurrection—as One risen—he embraces the dead and the living, and takes them with him on his way to the consummation of God's kingdom. If I understand it rightly, this means that the dead are dead and not yet risen, but they are already "in Christ" and are with him on the way to his future. When he appears in glory, they will be beside him and will live eternally with him. That is what Paul means too when he says that "neither death nor life...will be able to separate us from the love of God that is in Christ Jesus" (Rom. 8.38f.), for the unconditional and prevenient love of God is the beginning of the divine glory that raises the dead and annihilates death. (1996, 105)

When Moltmann interprets resurrection to eternal life in this way, it lends credence to the funeral seen as an eschatological assembly, as discussed in chapter 6. Just as the act of assembling is an eschatological symbol, in which the people participate in the truth and hope associated with the crucified and risen Christ, so the resurrection symbol expressed in the funeral liturgy is eschatological. In this sense, it is like a spotlight directing the attention of the assembled people of God to the deceased, making specific the more general and unspoken eschatological symbolism associated with the act of assembling for worship.

Consequently, the incorporation stage of a Christian funeral also relates to the mourners. In this respect, it would make good sense for Protestant Christians to serve the Lord's supper in funerals. There could hardly be a more profound rite of incorporation than holy communion.

Conclusion

Caring for the bereaved through funeral worship leadership is demanding. It places you in the position of having to address things we avoid thinking about most of the time. Accepting grief, facing death, and envisioning hope are spiritual challenges with which you must wrestle over time if you are to grow in your caring ministry to the bereaved through funerals. Learn to be content with your part in the funeral, and learn to live with uncertainty about the results of your care. Yet, have hope that something meaningful happens. In the next chapter, one meaningful result of Christian funerals will be discussed.

CHAPTER TEN

Funerals and Comfort

Comforting may be seen as something that helps a bereaved person be eased from pain for a time, whether through a hug or some kind of practical help such as babysitting the children for a couple of hours. It would be foolish to think that effective pastoral care practiced by ministers and church members means shying away from comforting in the pain-relieving sense. The very act of responding to a bereaved person in his or her hour of need can bring some kind of relief, regardless of what the minister or church member consciously intends. Nor does this mean that the grief process is being disrupted. Shock and denial are at work already, with or without the presence of the minister or church member, and these things are not a disruption of the grief process, they are its beginning. In fact, lack of comfort by the church, because of such things as not responding promptly, may create a lasting resentment in the heart and mind of a bereaved church member.

Comforting seems congruous with pre-funeral pastoral care, because caring for the bereaved before the funeral provides the opportunity for personal conversation and practical helping acts. For instance, reminiscing about the deceased may bring laughter and reflection. But it is hard to think of a funeral bringing comfort rather than being something to dread or something that you just have to get through. Before the funeral, you may think that relief will come when it is over. So there must be another way of understanding comfort if it is to have meaning for funerals.

Comfort in Funerals

This brings us to 1942, when a book on funerals was published titled *The Funeral: A Source Book for Ministers.* The author was pastoral theologian Andrew Blackwood, a professor at Princeton Theological Seminary who chaired what was then known as the practical department.

Blackwood began his fifth chapter by citing some purposes for holding a Christian funeral. His first purpose was that the funeral should glorify God. But immediately he qualified this answer by saying that the best way to glorify God in the presence of death was to administer comfort. If he meant this merely in the pain-relieving sense, the funeral might very well be seen as something used inappropriately to help the bereaved avoid their grief. But this is not how he meant it. Instead, he went on to clarify what he did mean by comfort: "As the root idea of the word makes clear, to comfort means to strengthen in the Lord" (64).

Dictionary definitions of *comfort* clearly indicate that, although comfort may be understood in the pain-relieving sense, it first and foremost involves helping to strengthen someone, including moral or spiritual strengthening. According to *The Oxford English Dictionary,* to strengthen someone means "to give moral support, courage, or confidence to [a person]; to encourage, hearten, inspirit, fix in resolution." This understanding of comfort as strengthening is pretty clear cut, though multifaceted, and it suggests that comforting the bereaved in a funeral could be seen as occurring in a variety of ways, according to what different mourners need. One bereaved person might receive moral support, whereas another could gain needed courage or confidence. Still other mourners may discover encouragement, become heartened, or find resoluteness. On the whole, these things are future-oriented, providing something that will help the bereaved face the days, months, and years ahead as the grief process continues unfolding.

Yet, it is not at all clear how a funeral may accomplish such comfort, or whether this is what Blackwood meant by strengthening, which brings us to the second part of his definition of *comfort,* to strengthen "in the Lord." What Blackwood meant by "in the Lord" is indicated in his next sentence, which follows his definition of *comfort:* "Both in making the arrangements and in carrying them out, the pastor strives to bring the people into right relations with God, so that they will accept his plan for their altered lives" (64). In this understanding of "in the Lord," because this acceptance of God's plan is their comfort, it is God who does the actual comforting by providing a new plan for living. This could be seen as a kind of strengthening in the sense that the bereaved who accept God's plan may be encouraged and more confident that they have a future. At the same time, however, this view of comfort provides a real challenge to the bereaved. Being in right relation to God must involve discerning God's plan so that it can be accepted. Or, minimally, it means having faith that there is a plan, though it is not yet discerned. That seems like a tall order for a funeral.

Twelve years after Blackwood's book was published, Paul Irion discussed Blackwood's view of the purpose of a funeral in *The Funeral and the Mourners: Pastoral Care of the Bereaved* (1954). He called this view theocentric, "designed to undergird a belief in the sovereignty of God in death and life" (61), and he went on to note that comfort in this view "is seen as faith that even though God has brought to pass an alteration in life, he will provide the strength which is needed to assimilate the experience of loss" (61). In this interpretation of Blackwood, Irion shifted the theocentric focus and introduced a more psychological understanding of the bereaved. Instead of following what Blackwood wrote, that God has a plan for the altered life of the bereaved, Irion said that God brought about, or caused, the altered life. Although Irion observed that Blackwood was speaking "out of his Presbyterian heritage of Calvinism" (61), there still is a difference between God causing someone to become bereaved and God providing a new plan for living that the bereaved can embrace in faith.

Blackwood's view makes sense of comfort theologically understood, in the sense that there is a hopeful reason to turn to God. In Irion's interpretation, however, it is difficult to see why anyone would trust God's plan for his or her bereaved life. In fact, Irion did not say that comfort involves accepting a divine plan for living. Instead, he wrote that God provides some kind of "strength" that helps the bereaved to "assimilate the experience of loss." Now, the emphasis is shifted away from God's plan for living, except for a general faith in God's sovereignty, and is redirected toward God helping the bereaved embrace a different plan for living described psychologically as assimilating the experience of loss. Irion went on to summarize his view this way: "We can say, then, that one of the purposes of the funeral is to relate people to God in such a way that they can draw upon the resources of God's spirit in their hour of confusion and need" (61).

Whatever their differences, both Blackwood and Irion saw comfort as the means of achieving the main purpose of the funeral understood theologically. There is, however, another way to view comfort that may occur in a funeral, one that is consistent with caring through funerals by facilitating mourning.

Comfort: A Possible Result of Mourning in Funerals

According to Blackwood, one purpose of a funeral is to glorify God, but he does not elaborate on this. Instead, he moves quickly to the means of accomplishing this purpose, which he describes in terms of comfort. Rather than following Blackwood here, let's take a step back and begin at the point of explicitly identifying the kind of funeral under consideration, because this will determine the purpose.

Initially, what is needed is an explicit statement that the kind of funeral being discussed is a Christian funeral, as opposed to funerals in other religions, and as opposed to nonreligious funerals. It is important to be up front about this, because it is the main thing that determines the purpose of the funeral. Of course, Blackwood presupposes that he is referring to a Christian funeral when he uses the language of glorifying God, and, likewise, Irion presupposes this when he interprets Blackwood. Yet, it will be helpful for understanding funerals and comfort if we can be very explicit that the Christian funeral is the kind of funeral under discussion.

Now it becomes possible to say that the main purpose of a Christian funeral is to worship God. As we saw in chapter 6, the mourners engage in the symbolic act of assembling, or gathering, for worship. Part of this symbolic act includes mourners placing themselves in relation to truth and hope associated with the crucified and risen Christ. They bring their real situations of bereavement to the assembly, and they may include remembrance of the deceased as part of the worship.

This brings us to the question of how the purpose of worshiping God in a Christian funeral is accomplished. Once again, it becomes necessary to diverge from Blackwood and Irion. It is not comfort that accomplishes this purpose, even in a funeral. Rather, it is doing such things as praying, singing, hearing the scriptures read, and listening to the sermon that accomplishes the purpose of the funeral. In other words, participation in the funeral liturgy is the means of accomplishing the purpose of worshiping God in a Christian funeral.

Comfort, then, is not a means of accomplishing the purpose of the funeral. Rather, comfort seen as the strengthening of mourners according to ways they need to be strenghtened is a possible result of assembling to worship God through participation in the funeral liturgy.

Ministers and Comfort

If only the pastor can strive hard enough, surely the mourners will be comforted. If only this were true! But there is no one-to-one correlation between the effort you put into the funeral and the potential results that the mourners may experience. Instead, your contribution to comfort is more modest. Although you contribute to the comfort of the mourners by preparing the funeral liturgy and leading the funeral worship service, some may not experience comfort. Following one funeral at which I officiated, several church members were very complimentary to me, and one or two remarked that they wanted their funeral to be just like this one. Naturally, hearing this made me feel good. However, as if to ensure that I would not think too highly of myself, a relative of the deceased sent me a letter a few days after the funeral that quickly cut me down to size. This relative was hopping mad about the funeral, because it did not contain the type of content that this person thought it should contain for honoring the beloved dead relative properly. This person was not a member of the congregation but was in a very different denomination. And, in reality, what this person experienced in the funeral was a clash of liturgical traditions. The moral of this story is that it is best to be humble in what you think you can accomplish in a funeral, even in the realm of comfort.

This being said, within the context of your liturgical tradition, your funeral preparation and worship leadership do make a difference. You make a difference through the choices you make when preparing the funeral liturgy and by enabling the mourners to participate in that liturgy through your worship leadership. In chapters 6 and 7, it became apparent that funeral liturgies tend to be flexible and adaptable. There are options throughout the liturgy. In conjunction with requests made by the bereaved family, the minister determines the order of worship and, within that, chooses one scripture passage rather than another, one prayer rather than another, one song rather than another, one emphasis in the sermon rather than another and omits or includes one part of the liturgy rather than another to fit the circumstance.

Having choices raises the question of the basis on which those choices are made. The first part of the basis is your liturgical tradition, which gives you a particular set of options. Within this context, the second part of the basis is your knowledge of the bereaved coming from pre-funeral encounters with them. Whether this knowledge is extensive or minimal, it is what enables you to use your tradition and understanding of grief fruitfully. This can be seen in the situation in which Rev. Jordan found herself when she received a request to conduct the funeral of a man named John.

A Comforting Funeral

Rev. Jordan actually had met John and his family three weeks earlier when she was preparing to conduct the funeral of his mother, Grace, a woman she had known for several years. At the time of his mother's death, John was undergoing tests as a hospital patient. He did attend his mother's funeral, but returned to the hospital immediately afterward. His disease was diagnosed two weeks later, but it was too late. Tragically, he died the day after he received the diagnosis, at fifty-eight.

Thirty to forty people were at the funeral, including John's brother, Mark, his sister, Marie, and his ex-wife, Rachel. The divorce between Rachel and John, who had been married for twenty years, had become final a few weeks earlier, after John had become hospitalized. Rev. Jordan found herself characterizing the brother, sister, and ex-wife not only as exhausted from the illness, death, and funeral of John's mother but also now as emotionally "raw" in the aftermath of John's untimely death. They seemed like wires in an old cord whose outer protective skin has been split open, no longer shielding them.

Rev. Jordan allowed her knowledge of their bereavement to guide her funeral preparation, as she wondered how their participation in the liturgy possibly could have a comforting result. Might God strengthen them through this means? Her thinking about this took a step forward due to the family's two requests for the funeral. Because the two deaths were so close together, the family members wanted a piece of music from their mother's funeral played at the beginning of John's, and they wanted Psalm 23 read, as it had been at the mother's funeral.

Linking the two funerals in these ways got Rev. Jordan to thinking about John in the family context, especially in relation to other family members who had died, including his recently deceased mother and his father, who died years ago. Because of her prior relationship with the mother, Rev. Jordan knew that her husband had been an alcoholic who always had trouble holding a job. John, as the oldest of the children, did not have an easy time growing up in this family. Now Mark, Marie, and Rachel would have old family wounds surface once more.

At this point, Rev. Jordan found herself resisting going further in the funeral preparation, but she was not sure why. Time was short, and she had no opportunity to set the funeral aside and return to it later. From experience, she had learned that sometimes her resistance to going further involved something from her own life intruding on the task at hand and disrupting it. So she did something that she had done many times before in such situations: She prayed. But this was not a prayer of many words; it was a prayer of listening for what wanted to emerge from within. Before long, she remembered a funeral in her own family, in particular the minister who preached the sermon. As she reflected on this, she realized that it did not have to do with her grief from the past, but with a situation with which she was wrestling in her present church. What she remembered about the minister from the funeral was that he neglected her at a time when she really needed to feel included in what was going on in relation to the death and funeral of the family member. Then she had an anxious thought about the present—that some of the church members involved in the troubling situation possibly were feeling the same way about her, that she was neglecting them at a time when they really needed to feel included. As valuable as this thought probably would turn out to be, Rev. Jordan realized she would have to delay dealing with it further until after the funeral. Now she hoped that, having acknowledged this intrusion, she would be able to finish preparing the funeral, which turned out to be the case.

Rev. Jordan decided on a theme of God's comfort for the funeral liturgy. She knew quite well that making divine comfort an explicit focus in the funeral would not in any way guarantee a comforting result. Instead, this is what came to her intuitively in response to the rawness of the family's bereavement.

This theme was made explicit in the scripture readings and in the sermon. Psalm 23 fit well, with its emphasis on divine shepherding:

"Even though I walk through the darkest valley, I fear no evil; for you are with me; your rod and your staff–they comfort me" (v. 4). Likewise, the Old Testament reading that Rev. Jordan chose was a very familiar funeral passage, Isaiah 40:1–11, 28–31. It begins: "Comfort, O comfort my people, says your God" (v. 1). It goes on to contrast the finitude of humanity, portrayed as grass, with the eternity of God: "The grass withers, the flower fades; but the word of our God will stand forever" (v. 8). Then verse 11 echoes the divine shepherding of Psalm 23: "He will feed his flock like a shepherd; he will gather the lambs in his arms, and carry them in his bosom, and gently lead the mother sheep." Finally, verses 28–31 emphasize that God's power and strength yield very encouraging results, in which the people are strengthened: "but those who wait for the Lord shall renew their strength, they shall mount up with wings like eagles, they shall run and not be weary, they shall walk and not faint" (v. 31).

The comfort theme readily expressed in these Old Testament passages continues in the New Testament passages that Rev. Jordan chose, but now the focus is on Christ. The first New Testament reading is another familiar funeral passage, Romans 8:31–39. In the second part of verse 31, Paul asks, "If God is for us, who is against us?" He goes on to conclude that nothing can separate us from the love of God in Christ: "For I am convinced that neither death, nor life, nor angels, nor rulers, nor things present, nor things to come, nor powers, nor height, nor depth, nor anything else in all creation, will be able to separate us from the love of God in Christ Jesus our Lord" (vv. 38–39). If God is a comforting shepherd, Christ shows that God's strength is unmatchable and that God's divine love is undefeatable. Therefore, God is eternally trustworthy.

The second reading shifts to a very different imagery. It includes selected verses from Revelation 21–22, about a new heaven and a new earth that replaces the old heaven and earth, which have passed away. Chapter 21 begins with the author seeing a new Jerusalem descend from heaven. Then a voice from the throne says:

> See, the home of God is among mortals.
> He will dwell with them;
> they will be his peoples,
> and God himself will be with them;
> he will wipe every tear from their eyes.
> Death will be no more;
> mourning and crying and pain will be no more,
> for the first things have passed away. (vv. 3–4)

Chapter 22 concludes the vision of the new Jerusalem with a description of "the river of the water of life" (v. 1) flowing from the throne of God and of the Lamb through the middle of the city street. On either side of the river is the "tree of life" (v. 2), whose leaves are for the healing of the nations. Nothing accursed will be in the city, nor will there be any night: "And there will be no more night; they need no light of lamp or sun, for the Lord God will be their light, and they will reign forever and ever" (v. 5). Finally, toward the end of the chapter, there is an invitation to all who dwell in the city to drink the water of life: "Let anyone who wishes take the water of life as a gift" (v. 17).

Rev. Jordan drew on these passages in Revelation for her sermon:

Introduction. She began by making some personal remarks about John. Because she did not know him well, she shared some positive things that family and friends had told her about him, such as when he spoke words of concern for his sister before he died, showing that he never stopped being a caring person who loved his family.

Heaven. In the next part of the sermon, she shared something she had learned from a seminary professor years ago, that there are different visions of heaven and that it's not so important to have any particular one as long as you have one. She went on to illustrate by telling the congregation that when she was younger, her vision of heaven was that "we don't know what happens, but we trust God to take care of us." "However," she said, "as I have grown older and have lost more people to death, I have found comfort, God's strength, in the image of heaven as a place where we are together with the people we love and with God." She then told about an experience she had several years earlier. One day she was having a pre-baptismal conference with a church member

> whose losses had brought him back to church to have his three children baptized. During the course of conversation about lost loved ones, I told him about two of my closest family members who had died, my brother Ron and my uncle James with whom I spent many hours growing up, and said, "If I could be with them again, it would just be heaven." His eyes filled with tears, and he nodded and said, "Yes, it would just be heaven."

Having given these examples, she related them to the Revelation passages and to John and his mother.

> It is comforting for me to envision John and Grace together in God's care and presence, and so I offer that vision to you–that no matter where they are and what form they are in, they are together and they are at peace. The words of Revelation say that there is no more pain or tears or grief in the beautiful city with a river flowing through it with blooming trees growing on either side. And the tree of life has leaves that are for the healing of the peoples.

Every funeral sermon is unique in the sense that, to some extent, it emerges from the preacher's encounter with the bereaved, and often from a relationship with the one who died. In this instance, Rev. Jordan responded to the bereaved family's rawness by taking the sermon beyond a focus on relief from pain to strengthening.

Healing. Rev. Jordan introduced the need for healing in the next part of her sermon as she told about an encounter she had with John in the hospital one day before his mother's death. "When I visited John the day before his mother died, he told me he was afraid of what was happening to his body, afraid that no one could figure out what was wrong with him. And, then he said, 'I guess I should just trust God with this. I should put myself in God's hands.' Then, we prayed together."

Naturally, John wanted his body to be healed. But, this was not the only thing Rev. Jordan had in mind as she unfolded the emphasis on healing. Before the funeral, John's brother, Mark, had told Rev. Jordan his biggest regret about John's death. It had to do with alcoholism in the family. John had not come to a place of healing and reconciliation with his alcoholic family, and it made Mark angry that he had died before finding the healing he needed. It was this, as much as the need for John's physical healing, that she had in mind as she continued, "When we are born, we come into this world new, fresh and shiny, and then the world has its way with us. We are wounded and need to be healed." Upon saying this, Rev. Jordan told a brief story about a childhood wound and the need for healing found in *The Child's Song: The Religious Abuse of Children*, by Donald Capps, in which the author tells about a family experience he had as a child. She began the story, saying,

> His younger brother, who was four years old, had been difficult that day. After dinner, the parents took the family for a drive, but their destination was not a pleasant one. They drove to a local orphanage, stopped the car, and acted as if they were going to leave the little four-year-old there because of his behavior. Horrified, Capps pleaded with his parents: "Don't send him away. He'll be good. Just give him a second chance." (1995, 170)

Then she read a lengthy quote from Capps's adult reflection on this critical childhood event:

> For a very long time–months, maybe even years–I assumed that my parents were capable of abandoning a child of theirs, and I did all in my power to make certain that it would never be me. But something surely died in me–in all of us–that night. Life before that night had not been perfect. There had been the usual conflicts between parents and children, the usual fighting and

reconciliation. But this was different. This was the threat of abandonment. The sense of dread that this threat produced in me was nearly overwhelming...

And yet, even though I know now that it was not my pleadings that saved him, I believe, nonetheless, that there was wisdom in my contention that he should be given a "second chance." The original Garden of Eden story undermines this belief and, in so doing, leaves us feeling demoralized, as though we have been condemned to live in a world in which all of us must get perfect marks and any mistake or failure means that we are condemned for life. The author of Revelation also challenges the story, as he envisions all the children of the world gathering beside the river where stands the tree of life, with its twelve kinds of fruit and its healing leaves (Rev. 22:2).

Which is to say that the Bible itself, this book of our lives, this book that Augustine took up and read when he came to that moment in his life when he desperately needed a second chance, envisions our return to the garden, there to reexperience the inner peace that surpasses all understanding, a deep satisfaction with the self that we are, a profound gratitude for our one and only life and those who made it possible, and a wide embrace of the whole created order of things. The song of the soul. (170–71)

After she finished reading this extended quote, Rev. Jordan said, "That would just be heaven. That is the heaven I envision for John and for Grace, the garden where there is the second chance, where healing can be completed and they live forever in God's peace. This image strengthens me for what lies ahead, and I offer it to you in the hope that it may strengthen you, too."

Conclusion. For the ending of the sermon, Rev. Jordan read aloud Revelation 22:1–5:

Then the angel showed me the river of the water of life, bright as crystal, flowing from the throne of God and of the Lamb through the middle of the street of the city. On either side of the river is the tree of life with its twelve kinds of fruit, producing its fruit each month; and the leaves of the tree are for the healing of the nations. Nothing accursed will be found there any more. But the throne of God and of the Lamb will be in it, and his servants will worship him; they will see his face, and his name will be on their foreheads. And there will be no more night; they need no light of lamp or sun, for the Lord God will be their light, and they will reign forever and ever.

After the funeral worship ended, and the mourners had been to the cemetery, they gathered at a restaurant for a meal. There was a brief time of waiting for the tables to be prepared, so the group was standing around talking. It was during this time that John's sister, Marie, approached Rev. Jordan and said, "I didn't expect to find any comfort in this service, but I did."

A few minutes later, a close friend of the family, whose name was Peter, introduced himself to Rev. Jordan. He thanked her for making the tie between comfort and strength. Then he told her that he had a certain form of cancer and went on to explain that linking these two things was helpful to him in his effort to cope with his illness.

After this, it was time for everyone to be seated. Rev. Jordan was asked to say the blessing.

Mourners and Comfort

As an experienced minister, Rev. Jordan took the comments of Marie and the family friend in stride. She was glad the funeral worship was helpful to these two mourners, but she also knew that there were many other people at the funeral, and she would never know how any of them responded. Nevertheless, she did file away in her mind an observation she made from the two comments. It was that comfort may be different for different mourners based on the particular kind of strength needed.

Different Mourners

For Marie, perhaps the wound of her rawness was beginning to heal so that she genuinely could grieve. It may be that the leaves on the tree of life in the vision of the new Jerusalem were for her, and not only for her dead brother. Because the vision of heaven she encountered in the funeral liturgy did not deny family wounds and the need for healing, but instead incorporated all of this into the image of a reconciled and healed family, perhaps she too was reconciled in some way in her own soul. Perhaps, with the edge taken off her emotional rawness, it was just a little easier for her to begin coming to grips with the reality of her mother's death and of her brother's death, so that she would have less need of denial in the days to come.

For the family friend, Peter, the situation was different. The strength he gained from his encounter with the funeral liturgy could not have been the same as it was for Marie. In addition to his grief over the loss of his friend, John, he was wrestling with cancer. When Rev. Jordan told about her conversation with John in the hospital on the day before his mother died, John's words may have resonated with his grieving friend. Perhaps, like John, Peter feared what was happening to his body and thought that he too would like to put his situation in God's hands. Perhaps, strengthening for him was that he gained courage both to face his fear and to trust in God more intentionally than he had up to this point.

Different Parts of the Liturgy

Just as the differing situations of mourners prevent all comfort from being the same, so some mourners may be comforted in relation to different parts of the liturgy than others. As we saw at John's funeral, the sermon was important for comforting. However, it can just as well be a passage of scripture, a hymn, or any other aspect of the liturgy that contributes to comfort.

In one funeral, a song was especially meaningful to many mourners. When the pastor met with the family to discuss the funeral of their mother, her middle-aged son made an unusual request. He wanted the song "Over the Rainbow," made famous by Judy Garland in *The Wizard of Oz,* sung as a solo. The minister's initial reaction was not favorable. However, when the son told why he made this request, the song was put in a different light, and it became a meaningful part of the funeral in which the mourners could participate and potentially receive comfort.

Years ago, when the son was a teenager still living at home with his parents, he had an experience that changed his perception of his mother. His father had been laid off from work, and his mother worked the night shift—and occasionally double shifts—to help make ends meet. This situation continued long enough that she became exhausted, and sometimes she looked depressed. One evening, the son came downstairs and just happened to see his mother watching television. There was nothing unusual about this, but something caught his attention. His mother was watching the Judy Garland show, and Garland was singing "Over the Rainbow." In this moment, the son suddenly perceived his mother differently than ever before. She was no longer just his mother, who did the usual things that mothers do for their teenage sons. Instead, he saw her as a person, a human being in her own right, an individual who had her own hopes and dreams and who yearned for better times. The song "Over the Rainbow" took on the significance of expressing the hopeful yearnings of this woman yet to be fulfilled. In the funeral, right before the commendation, the son told this story about his mother, and then the song was sung as a solo.

Memory and Comfort

Because comfort through participation in a funeral liturgy is so subjective, and because so few people ever talk about their subjective reactions in funerals, most comfort may remain undisclosed to the minister or to others. Yet, there is a way that comfort sometimes is discussed, often months or even years after the funeral—an indirect way in which the mourner remembers one or more specific parts of the funeral that stood out and seemed meaningful. This part of the funeral liturgy has never been forgotten, even though literally nothing else from the funeral can be remembered. If you ask people to explain what is meaningful about that part which is remembered, they end up talking about how it helped them, spoke to them, or captured a valued quality of the deceased so beautifully. In short, the person is talking about being comforted through participation in that part of the funeral liturgy.

In a book on grief titled *Ministering to the Grief Sufferer* (1964), the author, pastoral counselor C. Charles Bachmann, interviewed a woman whose husband had died suddenly ten months earlier. During the course of talking about her experience, she described her effort to accept her husband's death:

> It's hard to point to a time when I really accepted it. I'm not so sure I have made that stick...You say: "Thy will be done," and then things begin to happen; you have to be careful what you ask the Lord for...Death is not the worst thing; there are things that are worse...But life goes on, nobody can really reassure you, you have to believe there is more to life than existence here. (52)

Next, she brought the funeral into the discussion, citing the one part of the liturgy she remembered and how it helped her: "Nothing I read helped very much, you just have to accept it...At first I asked why? why? and no answers came...The Twenty-third Psalm was so calming. It was used in the funeral service. It was the only thing I remember about the funeral service...I kept using it over and over again" (52). This woman's funeral encounter with Psalm 23 proved to be comforting in the sense of calming her during a significant time following the funeral, as she returned to it repeatedly when she was trying to accept her husband's death and was asking the difficult question, "Why?"

There even are times when the act of assembling for the funeral provides comfort and becomes a lasting memory. At the beginning of my grandfather's funeral, discussed in chapters 8 and 9, his men's Sunday school class filed into the sanctuary and sat together in the front row on the right, across from my family, who sat on the left side. He had been a part of this class since I was a child, and seeing their familiar faces brought back memories from my childhood. At the time, seeing them was comforting to me in the sense of affirming the value of my grandfather's life. However, as I reflect on this today, the memory of their assembling seems far more comforting to me now than it did then, in the sense of providing me with a hopeful image. Their assembling bears witness to an important possibility for a person's life in the church. This possibility, it seems to me, includes being part of a group that takes spiritual development seriously through the study of scripture, bears one another's burdens, and nurtures lasting friendships.

It may seem that this says more about the present circumstance of my life than it does about my grief, because my grandfather died so long ago. Nevertheless, it does suggest that memories of the funeral can play a meaningful, comforting role in the lives of those who mourn.

Finally, in some instances there are negative funeral memories, and these may be more difficult to face. Yet, even these may contain the seed of comfort, indirectly, if they can be faced courageously. Recall, from chapter 8, the adult children who had been told that their father was going to hell because he committed suicide. I am not suggesting that underneath this is something positive. Rather, when their mother died several years later, the present pastor helped them begin reinterpreting their father's death. Facing a negative funeral memory contains the possibility of becoming freed from its harmful influence on your life. If you are remembering a negative funeral memory years after the fact, you bring the possibility of reinterpretation, greater wisdom born of experience, and the opportunity to forgive.

Conclusion

Comfort is one possible caring result of a Christian funeral. Through participating in the funeral liturgy, mourners may be strengthened in ways meaningful to them at the time. But a remembered part of the funeral also may be a continuing source of strength in the future.

CHAPTER ELEVEN

Pastoral Care After the Funeral

The funeral is over. It is business as usual again, with an exception. Neither you, the family, nor friends of the deceased have finished grieving, which raises an important question. As pastor, what do you do next? This chapter is about caring for the bereaved during the first few days and weeks following the funeral, as opposed to the long-term pastoral care that extends through the entire course of the grief process. When pastoral care following the funeral is discussed in this chapter, it refers only to the very first caring encounters that the minister has with the bereaved after the funeral.

Those Who Receive Pastoral Care After the Funeral

Assuming there was more than one bereaved person at the funeral, determining who receives the pastor's caring attention after the funeral is the post-funeral corollary to the same issue discussed in chapter 3 about who receives pre-funeral pastoral care from the minister. Normally, the same family members who made funeral arrangements and were visited by the minister before the funeral receive care from the pastor after the funeral. It may be a widow or widower, a parent or child, a grandparent, or other relatives. If the deceased was single, it may be a partner with whom the deceased lived, or it may be a close friend if the deceased lived alone. In any case, the field normally is narrowed to church members who live in the community, though of course there are always exceptions.

Next, there is the reality that the minister of the church remains the minister of others in the church who may be grieving the loss of the deceased, along with the family. These bereaved church members may appear to be providing the primary lay care in support of the bereaved family, having been longtime friends of the deceased and other family members, or they may have been in a church group with the deceased for several years. Is it possible to care for friends of the deceased who are church members, or even for whole groups of bereaved people in the church?

Finally, there is your grief. If you had a relationship with the deceased church member, surely you have some grief reaction. How then do you receive care following the funeral, when you grieve the loss along with others?

As you can see, from the standpoint of pastoral ministry, caring for the bereaved following the funeral is not as simple as it would be if there were only one identified grieving person. Instead, the bereaved needing care during the days following the funeral may include not only the family but other church members and yourself as well.

Caring for the Bereaved After the Funeral

In pastoral ministry, caring for the bereaved after the funeral continues to involve facilitating mourning. Again, facilitating mourning simply means helping bring about mourning, only this time it is post-funeral mourning.

You might be tempted to assume that, because the funeral is over, mourning now exists only in relation to the grief process. However, this is not the case for church members. For them, mourning following the funeral includes two additional events, both of which can be viewed as post-funeral rites of incorporation.

The first one is the pastoral follow-up visit with the bereaved family after the funeral. The second is when the bereaved family returns to church following the funeral. Although the focus is on the bereaved family members in both these events, the second one includes other church members who are grieving. Finally, though you are the worship leader, this time may be especially meaningful for you as well.

The Follow-up Visit

At some point during the week following the funeral, it is a good idea for the minister to call the family on the phone and make an appointment to visit. When to call, and when to visit, will vary with circumstances. For instance, one funeral was on a Friday. Adult children of the surviving spouse were staying with their parent through Sunday afternoon, when they were scheduled to return to their homes in other cities. It was appropriate for the minister to give the family some time together during the weekend, before making a phone call to schedule a visit.

The minister made the phone call on the following Wednesday, clearly stating the purpose for the call. The widow said that she would like a visit, and a time was set for the following Tuesday. This was a busy time for the woman. She had a doctor's appointment to keep, along with several other appointments. Any notion that bereaved family members are just sitting around waiting for the minister to drop in is sheer romantic fantasy from the past.

You may visit fairly quickly in some cases, whereas in others you may not visit for two or three weeks. Just be sure that you make the phone call within a reasonable amount of time according to the circumstances, be clear about the purpose for visiting, and have your calendar there so that you can schedule a time for the visit.

The follow-up visit is not for the purpose of beginning a counseling relationship with the bereaved family. Instead, your visit is a rite that involves the family being reincorporated into the church community as a grieving family, and as grieving individuals. As pastor, you represent the church community in this visit, and what you are conveying through the visit is that both you and the church community accept the family members in their new status as a grieving family every bit as much as they were accepted before the death.

On the phone, you may say something as simple as, "I would just like to see how you're doing." The visit itself may seem like a typical pastoral care visit in which you have conversation ranging over several areas of the situation. Yet, through this conversation, you are establishing contact with a family that is living in the new reality of grief.

This rite also is important for you. By visiting, you are resisting any desire you may have to avoid the grieving family so that you will not have to face your own grief or any fear you may have about encountering grief in others due to uncertainty. Once you get to know what it is like, you can be more confident. Moreover, just as the status of the family has changed, so your ministry has changed, because you now are showing that you can be the pastor of this family, which requires that you be able to relate to them as grieving people.

The First Sunday Back

In the example earlier, the widow did not come to church on the Sunday following the funeral. However, she did return on the second Sunday, which was before the scheduled pastoral visit. If, however, the visit had occurred before the bereaved woman had returned to church, it could have been discussed in the visit. You can bring it up, if the one being visited does not mention it. If nothing else, breaking the ice with regard to this subject provides an opportunity for conversation about it, which can help the family muster their courage to return when they are ready.

The first Sunday back can be a very emotionally difficult time for the bereaved family. Some fear not being able to handle it and express a need for time before coming back. When they do return, some will sit up front rather than in their usual place, wheras others may slip in quietly, sit at the rear of the sanctuary, and then slip out quietly, hoping not to talk to anyone.

You, as the worship leader, are not immune from emotions when you see the family sitting there. Nor are other church members immune. The first Sunday back can be a significant event for many in the congregation, or even for the congregation as a whole in some instances.

This worship service is a rite of incorporation in which the grieving family is participating in the life of the church for the first time since the funeral, in their new situation of being grieving family members. It is a time when the congregation as a whole shows acceptance of the family in their newfound situation of grieving. If others in the church also are grieving the loss, it can be a rite of incorporation for them as well, though the focus will not be on them. Rather, as part of their mourning, they will be showing acceptance and giving support as members of the church community.

If you are aware that the family members are making their return on a particular Sunday, it influences your worship preparation. This worship service is neither a second funeral nor a memorial service. Rather, because the family is returning to life in the church community following the funeral, it is appropriate that this be a normal worship service. Yet, it can be a worship service that is sensitive to the mourners. A statement of condolence may be written in the bulletin. One hymn may seem better than another for the occasion. One emphasis may seem timelier than another in the sermon. However, the most important part of the worship liturgy for addressing the mourning directly is the pastoral prayer, which should include a time of praying for the grieving family and for all who grieve. An exception to this is when the congregation has been traumatized, and the sermon, as well as the whole service, will be focused on the bereavement situation.

In chapter 8, we saw that mourning provides a bridge connecting the funeral and the first phase of grief. Following the funeral, mourning continues providing this bridging function for church members. On one side of the bridge are the two rites of incorporation, including the follow-up visit and the first Sunday back. On the other side is grief, potentially in the earliest part of its second phase. Let's cross the bridge to grief in order to see how the rites of incorporation may interact with it.

Grief and Mourning After the Funeral

Those who grieve, having made it out of the starting gate, have most of the race yet to run. The bulk of the grief process lies ahead after the funeral. Seen from your standpoint as the minister of the church, your practice of pastoral care with the bereaved requires that you get to know the second phase of the grief process as it unfolds following the funeral, along with the mourning processes associated with it, just as you needed knowledge of phase one.

Introducing the second phase of the grief process may give the impression that there is a neat transition from phase one to phase two following the funeral. It would be presumptuous, however, to make this assumption. It is far easier to describe the different phases of grief than to describe the transitions from one phase to another. The uniqueness individuals bring to grief seems especially pertinent here. One person lingers in one phase, another moves quickly from one to the other, and a third seems to be all over the map. Individual personalities, the relationship to the deceased, emerging secondary losses, and external circumstances are some of the things making the grief process seem unique to individuals. In addition, family dynamics play a role. Members of one family may be very emotionally expressive, whereas you would never know anyone had died in another family. The style of grieving may be tied up with intergenerational family dynamics (see Boszormenyi-Nagy and Spark, 1984).

There is another kind of uniqueness, not addressed in the psychological understanding of grief, which is seen commonly in churches. Within congregations are different generations of people, such as the Silent Generation, the Baby Boomers, Generation X, and the Millennials. Each generation has its unique character and ways of doing things, including ways of handling grief. For example, recall the case in chapter 5 when a minister and his spouse were murdered, resulting in congregational trauma. The judicatory of the congregation recommended that the interim pastor, who would be head of staff, serve for three years, and that the congregation not search for a new minister until the third year. It was felt that the church needed a year for healing followed by a thorough study of its mission. Some key church members reacted negatively to this plan, because they viewed this strategy as tantamount to treading water. Instead, the church needed to "get on with it" (Hudson, 1998, 27).

The executive presbyter, Jill Hudson, went to talk to these vocal critics, who were members of a weekly men's prayer breakfast. As she spoke about the reasons for the plan, she noticed that most of the men were from the generation that fought World War II. After finding out that most of them served in the war, she named the way they had learned to cope with grief during wartime: "I pointed out that in combat when a buddy was injured or killed, they had to keep going–the stakes were so high that they couldn't afford to stop and grieve. I suggested that this pattern of bucking up and moving ahead was a learned one that had served them well in battle. Heads nodded in agreement" (27–28).

Next, she pointed out that many in the congregation never had that war experience, and they needed a different way to cope with their grief: "For these individuals, grief had a different dynamic. They couldn't go on until the emotional issues were addressed. I told the story of a woman who, eight weeks after the violent death, was still frightened to get up during the night and would awaken her husband before leaving the bedroom" (28).

Hudson offers a brief assessment of the situation and tells its outcome: "They had learned a generational response in a specific historical era, and it continued to determine their expression of grief and reaction to loss. With this understanding of the transitional period strategy, the prayer-breakfast participants became effective spokespeople for the board's decision" (28).

When ministers experience the ways that church members deal with their grief, they should take generational differences into account, along with cultural, gender, racial, and ethnic differences. When all these things are added to the mix, it becomes exceedingly evident that the ways different people grieve and mourn are not all going to be the same or have the same meaning.

Another caution is that the second phase lasts for a long time, but this chapter is confined to a few days and a few weeks at most. It is about caring for those who are just getting started down the road of the second phase. Therefore, summarizing the second phase of grief can be misleading, and reading about it can be misleading, by giving the false impression that the second phase is collapsed into some short, easily identifiable time frame. So please read about the second phase of grief as a brief overview of what will be unfolding over a long period, well beyond a year typically, but which is only beginning just after the funeral.

A third caution is that the second phase, like other phases, is described in terms of acute grief. This may give you the impression that all mourners are devastated to the point of hardly being able to function in the world. Indeed, the final phase of grief describes the process of becoming involved in the world again fruitfully. In reality, the ways that grieving people lead their lives following the funeral are remarkably variable. Most people do not have the luxury of taking time off from work, or from school, and if they have a family, they must continue raising their children, who are part of the grieving family and continue leading their childhood lives of growing up. This is not to deny the painful reality of grief with which mourners must cope. Rather, it is to acknowledge that grieving people have to cope with the grief process as they lead their daily lives.

The Confrontation Phase of Grief

The name that Therese Rando gives to the second phase of grief is the confrontation phase. When the loss that the bereaved person wanted to avoid has been recognized, in the sense of going through the first phase of grief and mourning, the person now faces a new challenge, confronting the reality of the loss at a new level, which can bring intense pain. Authors often draw on the work of John Bowlby and Colin M.

Parkes for discussing this part of grief, and Rando is no exception. She briefly summarizes the confrontation phase using these two authors:

The confrontation phase is a time when grief is experienced most intensely and reactions to the loss are most acute. Separation from the loved one generates alarm in the mourner, which results in heightened autonomic arousal, anger, and protest and calls forth biologically based searching behavior. The mourner reacts to the strong urge to find, recover, and reunite with the lost one (see Bowlby, 1980, and Parkes, 1987). Pining or yearning (i.e., the persistent and obtrusive wishing and longing for the deceased) is the subjective and emotional component of the biological urge to search. This pining or yearning constitutes separation anxiety and is the characteristic feature of the pang of grief indicative of this time (Parkes, 1987, and Rando, 1993, 34).

The old saying "out of sight, out of mind" does not apply in this phase of grief. Instead, separation generates a protest against the loss, along with pining for the dead person. With this yearning comes searching, though to no avail. Searching ends in frustration, because the deceased person being sought cannot be found. However, there is something valuable being learned through this frustrating process: the dead loved one is irrevocably gone. Rando gives several examples:

> When the mourner hears a hilarious joke and reaches for the phone to pass it on to his brother, only to remember that his brother is buried across town, that painful realization teaches the mourner. When the bereaved mother hears the school bus but does not see her daughter step off of it, the searing agony she experiences teaches the mother. When the widow reaches out in the middle of the night to touch her husband, but her hand touches only air, her overwhelming loneliness teaches her. All such hurtful incidents teach the mourner the lesson he wants to resist—that the loved one is dead. (1993, 34)

According to Rando, this yearning and searching behavior will be repeated hundreds, or even thousands, of times, as the lesson being learned is appropriated gradually.

> Repeated frustration of desires for the deceased and the unsuccessful conscious and unconscious attempts to recover the loved one ultimately lead to a gradual diminution of disbelief and denial and then to the depression, disorganization, and despair that signal the mourner's relinquishment of hope for reversing the loss and avoiding his reactions to its reality. (1993, 34)

As this quote indicates, the confrontation phase can be an emotionally extreme time, in which the bereaved person may experience an unsettling variety of feelings. "It is an overwhelming, confusing, and frightening time as the mourner experiences types, intensities, and vacillations of emotions" (Rando, 1993, 35). But because individuals need relief from such emotional intensity, there also are psychological ways that bereaved human beings have of mitigating the emotions temporarily, such as experiencing a time of disbelief, avoiding reminders of the deceased, and selectively forgetting. Another form of mitigation is to find the deceased temporarily, through hallucinating, having a sense of the deceased's presence, or dreaming about the deceased (see 35). Finally, recall from chapter 3 that grief includes psychological, behavioral, social, and physical responses. There will be different configurations of these responses during the confrontation phase (see 35–40).

Though Rando describes the phase with acute grief in mind, this phase is relevant also for those whose grief would not be considered acute. Confrontation with the reality of death is important for all who grieve. Just as shock in the first phase can occur with different degrees of intensity, so the confrontation in the second phase can occur with varying degrees of emotional intensity. This brings us to mourning.

Mourning in the Confrontation Phase

Recall from chapter 2 that there are six R processes, or mourning processes, encompassing mourning from beginning to end. In this section, the second, third, and fourth R processes will be discussed briefly, because they correspond to the confrontation phase of the grief process, just as the first R process corresponds to the first phase of grief.

2. **React to the separation** (Rando, 1993, 47–48)

When the bereaved person has recognized the death, reactions to the separation from the deceased person can emerge. Mourning now involves allowing oneself to experience the reactions, express them, and cope with them.

Experience the pain (47). If protest and pining lead to searching for the lost loved one, the frustration of not finding the dead person, and having to face death's reality repeatedly, brings painful emotion. This emotion may have many vicissitudes. The type of emotion, its intensity, and its duration may vary dramatically among different people. Pain also may be felt across every dimension of grief, including its psychological, social, behavioral, and physical aspects. Ways of mitigating the pain of grief, mentioned above, also create opportunities for other positive aspects of mourning: "Respites and diversions permit distance and allow for replenishment, reconnection with other parts of life, and a renewed sense of control" (47). All these things allow the person to "carry on with mourning work; face the loss; and avoid the debilitation of constant, unremitting pain" (47). Yet, none of these things can be allowed to become so predominant that the pain of separation is avoided altogether. "Pain eventually must be felt" (47).

Feel, identify, accept, and give some form of expression to all the psychological reactions to the loss (47). Because pain can be so variable in the confrontation phase of grief, it is helpful to consciously allow for the different possibilities. Try to identify them and name them. Consider the possibility of relating different experiences to grief that might seem unrelated on the surface. Find ways of expressing painful experiences that are comfortable and appropriate.

Identify and mourn secondary losses (48). A host of secondary losses were mentioned in chapter 2 in the discussion of loss. Secondary losses highlight the long-term nature of the confrontation phase. Some secondary losses may emerge quickly after the death, such as the sudden lack of companionship. Others, however, may emerge after significant time has passed, such as expecting support during a crisis and finding that the characteristic support, which may have been present for years, is missing. Mourning includes identifying these experiences and letting them be part of the mix in the confrontation phase.

3. **Recollect and re-experience the deceased and the relationship** (Rando, 1993, 48–50)

The third R process moves from emphasizing the pain of separation to a focus on the relationship between the bereaved and the deceased. This is the same relationship discussed in the latter part of chapter 8. Rando even cites Irion (1966) on this (48). The purpose for this focus in the third part of mourning is that it helps the grieving person begin adapting to the physical absence of the dead loved one. "Over time, the mourner must discover new ways of relating to the deceased, the external world, and even herself. However, prior to this, the mourner must alter her emotional attachments to and investments in the loved one in order to make way psychologically for the subsequent changes" (48).

Review and remember realistically (49). In funerals, those who honor the deceased through sharing memories normally cast the dead person in a very positive light, most often to the exclusion of any negative qualities. If anything negative is mentioned, it is put in the context of a funny story or it is made to sound charming. This does not mean that the mourners are avoiding a realistic perception of the dead person. Rather, celebrating the life of the deceased is tied up with the fear of death and with recognizing finitude, so that highlighting the positive characteristics of the deceased is inevitable and appropriate. In the third mourning process, however, the purpose of focusing on the deceased is different. Time has passed since the funeral, and it becomes appropriate to include the negative, as well as the positive, aspects of the dead person when the mourner is remembering the deceased loved one and is reviewing the relationship over time.

The purpose of focusing on the relationship with the dead person is so that the mourner can change the emotional attachment that the mourner had with the deceased before the person died. This is part of what is needed if the mourner is to become able to form new, healthy, emotionally significant relationships in the future, and it is needed for forming a realistic, lasting memory of the dead person.

Revive and re-experience the feelings (49). One reason an attachment between two people is called an emotional attachment is that emotions form an important part of the connective tissue binding them together. Emotions associated with the deceased person must be allowed into the remembering and reviewing process mentioned previously, which enables them to be expressed in the context of remembering. This lessens their intensity and seemingly unending force, and they may even be spent, which allows ties to the deceased to be loosened. According to Rando, "Untying the ties does not mean that the deceased is forgotten or unloved. Rather, it means that the ties are modified to reflect the change that the loved one is now dead and cannot return the mourner's emotional investment or gratify her needs as before" (50).

4. **Relinquish the old attachments to the deceased and the old assumptive world** (50–52)

The fourth R process, or fourth mourning process, marks a shift from a focus on the relationship to the deceased to an important aspect of the mourner's own self, specifically what Rando calls the mourner's assumptive world. According to Rando, the assumptive world of a person "consists of all the assumptions (including expectations and beliefs) the individual sustains, with most of these becoming virtually automatic habits of cognition and behavior" (50). Some of the mourner's assumptions are global, pertaining to "the self, others, life, or the world in general" (51), whereas others are specific to the mourner's relationship to the deceased.

Both global and specific assumptions undergo an assault because of the death. For instance, the mourner's assumptive world may have included the specific expectation that the other person would always be there for the mourner. Now, that expectation is not valid and must be changed. This is only one example, but it could be multiplied endlessly, because "each of the ties the mourner has to the deceased is represented in his assumptive world" (51). These ties are associated with such things as needs, behaviors, wishes, interaction patterns, hopes, dreams, and beliefs. Because the dead person no longer can play a part in fulfilling these things, the assumptive world of the mourner is hopelessly out of date and must be revised. Otherwise, the mourner will be trapped in a "world of frustration and failed hopes for the loved one's return" (51).

It is not difficult to imagine that working through these three R processes takes time and is subject to many variables. Being aware of this, you can envision some of what you may be encountering when you interact with the bereaved in the months and years ahead, but this also has implications for pastoral care in the short term, after the funeral.

Grief, Mourning, and Pastoral Care
Following the Funeral

After the smoke has cleared from the funeral, conditions are right for the pining and searching behavior in the second phase of grief to become increasingly present, as the mourners return to their daily routines. Because the confrontation phase of the grief process will be unfolding for well beyond a year, the mourning processes associated with it also go far beyond the time of the two incorporation rites discussed above. Because the timing of those rites involves at most a few weeks beyond the funeral, it makes sense that the second R process is the most likely mourning process on which the mourner is focusing during this limited period. According to this mourning process, the grieving church member must begin reacting to the separation from the deceased upon experiencing frustration at not finding the dead loved one. The pain must be experienced, and its various manifestations must begin finding expression. At the same time, secondary losses are occurring, and they too must be mourned.

The follow-up visit and the return to church may be dreaded, because they require the grieving persons to focus on the deceased at the very time when pain associated with reacting to the separation may be increasing. During the visit, the bereaved may talk about what it has been like since the funeral and may talk about the dead loved one. During the worship service, there may be tears, or an emotional eruption at some point during the service. Returning to the church community goes hand in hand with pining and searching and the pain that it brings, though this may seem hidden in many instances.

There also may be secondary losses associated with the church. Now, a widow or widower, for instance, must come to church alone and learn how to relate to other members differently, as a single adult. The old, familiar, comfortable way of being at church is gone and must be mourned. Other mourning church members also may experience a secondary loss. For instance, the deceased spouse may have done some task in the church traditionally, such as collecting the bulletins after worship or setting up communion. Until church members mourn that loss, they may not handle finding someone else to perform the task very well. They may always associate the task with the deceased.

Finally, there is another way that the two post-funeral rites of incorporation and the grief process are related. If the grieving family can enter this new era of their life in the church community, in which they are accepted as grieving people, they will be putting themselves in the position of having the caring support of the church during the months and years to come, as the confrontation phase of grief unfolds.

Pastors know that their caring for the bereaved over time happens in the context of the church community, in conjunction with lay care. Many times, grieving church members will tell the pastor about friends in the church, or groups in the church, who have provided meaningful and helpful care over time.

Pastors know that most church members do not want formal counseling sessions, either in the home or in the pastor's office. One church member was very uncomfortable talking to the minister in his home. Yet, after church on Sunday, he would talk to the minister in detail about his life as a grieving widower on a regular basis over coffee. During the normal course of church life, the pastor may have informal caring conversations with the bereaved (see Bohler, 1996, 27–49, and Capps, 2001, on counseling conversations in congregations). If, during such conversations, the bereaved person says something indicating a pressing or extreme problem, such as "Pastor, I haven't slept in three days," it is appropriate for you to invite the person to make an appointment with you to talk further about the issue.

Finally, pastors know that grief does not happen for a few months and then is over. Trying to shoehorn a grieving church member into such a time frame for grief even could be harmful. Pastors have only to look at their own lives to know that.

The Pastor's Self-care

If you ever want to see what denial is like in the realm of grief, just talk to a pastor who conducts a fair number of funerals over a period of years. Such pastors may feel depressed, have physical problems, feel like crying at anything sentimental, not feel much joy, have marital or other relational difficulties, harbor secret desires to leave their work behind, drink too much, and feel that their interior life is turning to gelatin. But grief? Of course not. Better yet, talk to church leaders in the congregation. They may not have a clue about what is going on with their pastor. And even better than that, talk to the local church judicatory. They often are not informed about what is going on until it is too late.

Pastors who make denial a way of life do not skip a beat performing the rest of their work. They are right back at it after the funeral, or the morning after the funeral at the latest. It is a never-ending cycle of funerals and work. In this regard, pastors and churches do a dance of denial. The pastor never stops working, and the church expects the pastor to keep on keeping on. Neither churches nor pastors realize that funeral after funeral can have a cumulative effect, producing grief that may be profound but unrecognized. It strains credulity that pastors who conduct an average of several funerals per year, anywhere from two or three to ten or more, remain unaffected. Moreover, during this historical time when Protestant churches are aging and declining, whole congregations grieve as an ongoing part of their communal life.

It's not hard to guess that if you ever have a vulnerable moment and reveal how you feel to someone, the only thing they know to tell you is:

Go see a therapist. I do not disagree, depending on your particular situation. But seeing a therapist for support may not resolve your difficulty. I have an alternative that can work fairly quickly. Start allowing yourself to grieve and mourn along with everyone else! You will have to fight your denial, but you can do it! After a time, you will grow in your ability to interpret what you are experiencing as manifestations of grief, and you can allow it to be, rather than having to find ways of getting rid of it. You also can begin taking the R processes, or mourning processes, seriously. You may fear that you will break down at inappropriate times, but that is not true. You will be able to maintain control when you need to, and best of all, you will feel much better. You will be far more in touch with what grieving church members are experiencing. You will be able to identify their denial more easily, and your pastoral presence and wisdom will be more real and effective.

The second part of my alternative is that you let the governing board of your congregation in on your grief discovery and propose a plan for giving yourself more time to grieve and mourn following funerals. Taking time to grieve and mourn intentionally does not mean that you will become a lazy bum. Sometimes it may just mean that when you are alone in your office and you feel like crying, you allow yourself to cry, and you learn to identify your behavior as grief. If you will take just a little time for self-reflection, you may find yourself thinking about the funeral you did last week or last month, and you will become more comfortable realizing what is happening. It actually can be seen as a legitimate part of your ministry, in the sense that it allows you to cope effectively with your very emotionally difficult work, and it undoubtedly will increase your effectiveness in pastoral care with grieving church members. Moreover, there is theological fruit to be discovered if you go in this direction, and you even can begin planning a class on grief. You may have been looking for a topic for an adult class anyway, and why not this?

The third part of my alternative is more difficult and may need to be put off until you are feeling better. You need a different kind of support from your judicatory than you may be getting. The people in authority over you can do little more than refer you to a therapist, which is not the solution in this case. Here is what I propose. First, you must become an advocate for requiring your judicatory to provide a worship service for all pastors in the judicatory once a month, and if not once a month, at least once a quarter. In case you have not gotten the message yet, rites are extremely important for grief and mourning (see Vogel, 1996). Even psychologists are devising personal rites for grieving clients, so that they can move along in the grief process. If a worship service is provided for you, and you use enough self-discipline to actually attend it regularly, it can help you deal with your grief fruitfully. Is it not stunning that pastors rarely have the opportunity to sit in the pew and to worship!

Finally, you must become an advocate for peer group support. Notice that in seminary you probably learned little about grief or about group dynamics, and you became competitive with your peers, rather than learning to sit in groups with them for mutual support. You are darn lucky today if you have several compatible pastors in your area who form a support group for a few years before they move away. Why not become an advocate for requiring your seminaries to teach pastors how to support one another, and for requiring your judicatory to provide this. You need this support for your emotionally demanding work of conducting funerals and coping with your grief.

You may have noticed that in the previous section I indicated that the church community can provide grieving church members with caring support, and I did not exclude the minister from this. In the present section, however, I am focusing on the other side of the coin. Pastors and churches are not perfect, and their dance of denial can hinder effective pastoral care of the bereaved, both on the part of the pastor and on the part of the laity. Fortunately, this is not an all-or-nothing situation, on either side of the coin. Even though pastors often are in the peculiar position of conducting numerous funerals over a period of years, and even though they and the congregation may do a dance of denial, the church still can be a significant caring community for the bereaved. It will be a more effective caring community, however, if the pastor and church leadership can become proactive in fighting the denial and learning a different dance.

Conclusion

Caring for the bereaved following the funeral does not require abandoning ritual, or abandoning an understanding of pastoral care as facilitating mourning. It does, however, require a knowledge of the rites, mourning, and grief that occur following the funeral in the short term.

Because this book ends at the threshold of envisioning pastoral care of the bereaved in the long term, through the duration of the grief process, I would like to suggest several things essential for longer term pastoral care of the bereaved:

One is that pastoral care understood as facilitating mourning can continue to be a fruitful way to understand pastoral care throughout the grief process;

Second, mourning can continue to be seen as performing a bridging function between grief and the church throughout the grief process;

Third, the rites of the church, combined with the communal life of the church, can continue providing a far more effective means of caring for bereaved church members throughout the grief process than has been acknowledged in the past;

Fourth, pastors and churches need to grow in their understanding of the three phases of grief, and especially of the mourning processes associated with them;

Finally, pastors must make self-care a high priority, especially if they conduct funerals on a regular basis.

To sum it all up: A church whose pastor and members are people of sorrow is a healthier and more caring church than a church whose pastor and members are people of denial.

Postscript: Grief in a War-torn World

In the twentieth century, and now in the twenty-first century, whole societies have been swimming in death. World War I ensured that there was more than enough death and grief to go around the world in the twentieth century. Then of course there was World War II. And need anyone be reminded of the Holocaust? Oh yes, don't forget the atomic bomb, followed by the threat of global annihilation during the Cold War for almost the rest of the century, as well as the Vietnam War and the killing fields of Thailand. The slaughter continued with the Tiananmen Square massacre in China and genocide in Bosnia, Rwanda, and Kosovo. Lest we forget, there was the Gulf War, death squads in some South American countries, and hideously violent dictatorships. Now we mourn those who died on 9/11. Iraq was invaded, and the war on terrorism continues.

In the post-9/11 world, there is a serious need to reevaluate how society handles grief and mourning. Mid-twentieth century criticisms of the way society grieves and mourns are worthless at this point. If, in a war-torn world, people have difficulty grieving, it is not because they are not paying attention. It is not because they are superficial. It is not because cemeteries were moved away from churchyards, or because the funeral home business came into existence. It is because the world is traumatized by wars, violence, genocide, terrorism, and the continuing threat of global destruction.

If society sometimes copes through denial, that denial should be seen as an important part of grieving. It is for a sense of survival in the face of horrific realities seen globally through technology. The world desperately needs less violence over a long period if contemporary societies are to grieve and heal. Perhaps, for this reason, funeral rites play a more important part in society today than is generally recognized.

177

References

The American Heritage Dictionary of the English Language (1978). Boston: Houghton Mifflin Company.

Anderson, Herbert, and Foley, Edward (1998). *Mighty Stories, Dangerous Rituals: Weaving Together the Human and the Divine.* San Francisco: Jossey-Bass.

Backmann, C. C. (1964). *Ministering to the Grief Sufferer.* Englewood Cliffs, N.J.: Prentice-Hall.

Becker, Ernest (1973). *The Denial of Death.* New York: The Free Press.

Bell, Catherine (1997). *Ritual: Perspectives and Dimensions.* New York: Oxford University Press.

Blackwood, Andrew Watterson. (1942). *The Funeral: A Source Book for Ministers.* Philadelphia: The Westminster Press.

Bohler, Carolyn Stahl (1996). "Female-Friendly Pastoral Care." In *Through the Eyes of Women: Insights for Pastoral Care,* edited by Jeanne Stevenson Moessner. Minneapolis: Fortress Press.

Boszormenyi-Nagi, Ivan, and Spark, Geraldine M. (1984). *Invisible Loyalties: Reciprocity in Intergenerational Family Therapy.* New York: Brunner/Mazel.

Bowlby, John (1969). *Attachment.* Attachment and Loss, vol. 1. New York: Basic.

—— (1973). *Separation: Anxiety and Anger.* Attachment and Loss, vol. 2. New York: Basic.

—— (1980). *Loss: Sadness and Depression.* Attachment and Loss, vol. 3. New York: Basic.

Capps, Donald (1995a). *Agents of Hope: A Pastoral Psychology.* Minneapolis: Fortress Press.

—— (1995b). *The Child's Song: The Religious Abuse of Children.* Louisville: Westminster John Knox Press.

—— (2001). *Giving Counsel: A Minister's Guidebook.* St. Louis: Chalice Press.

Churches Participating in the Inter-Lutheran Commission on Worship (1978). *Lutheran Book of Worship: Ministers Desk Edition.* Minneapolis: Augsburg Publishing House, and Philadelphia: Board of Publication, Lutheran Church in America.

—— (1982). *Occasional Services: A Companion to Lutheran Book of Worship.* Minneapolis: Augsburg Publishing House, and Philadelphia: Board of Publication, Lutheran Church in America.

Damkroger, Brian (May 2001). "Conrad-Johnson Premier 17Ls line preamplifier." *Stereophile* 24, no. 5: 102.

Davies, J. G., ed. (1986). *The New Westminster Dictionary of Liturgy and Worship*. Philadelphia: The Westminster Press.

Episcopal Church (1979). *The Book of Common Prayer: and Administration of the Sacraments and Other Rites and Ceremonies of the Church: Together with The Psalter or Psalms of David: According to the Use of the Episcopal Church*. New York: Church Publishing.

—— (2000). *Enriching Our Worship 2: Ministry with the Sick or Dying, Burial of a Child*. New York: Church Publishing.

Fitzgerald, Helen (1994). *The Mourning Handbook: The Most Comprehensive Resource Offering Practical and Compassionate Advice on Coping with All Aspects of Death and Dying*. New York: Simon & Schuster.

Freud, Sigmund (1957). "Mourning and Melancholia." In *The Standard Edition of the Complete Psychological Works of Sigmund Freud*, vol. 14, edited and translated by. J. Strachey. London: Hogarth. (Original work published 1915.)

Fulton, Robert (1994). The Funeral in Contemporary Society. In *Death & Identity*, 3d ed., edited by R. Fulton and R. Bendiksen. Philadelphia: The Charles Press.

Gennep, Arnold van (1960). *The Rites of Passage*. Introduction by Solon T. Kimball. Translated by Monika B. Vizedom and Gabrielle L. Caffee. Chicago: The University of Chicago Press.

Glick, Ira O.; Weiss, Robert S.; Parkes, C. Murray (1974). *The First Year of Bereavement*. New York: John Wiley & Sons.

Hudson, Jill M. (1998). *Congregational Trauma: Caring, Coping and Learning*. Bethesda, Md.: Alban Institute.

Irion, Paul E. (1966). *The Funeral: Vestige or Value?* Nashville: Abingdon Press.

—— (1979). *The Funeral and the Mourners: Pastoral Care of the Bereaved*. Nashville: Abingdon Press. (Originally published in 1954 by Pierce & Washabaugh.).

Jackson, Edgar N. (1963). *For the Living*. Introduction by James A. Knight. Des Moines, Iowa: Channel Press.

Kline, Melanie (1940). "Mourning and Its Relation to Manic-Depressive States." *The International Journal of Psycho-Analysis* 21: 125–53.

Kübler-Ross, Elisabeth (1969). *On Death and Dying*. New York: MacMillan.

Lathrop, Gordon W. (1999). *Holy People: A Liturgical Ecclesiology*. Minneapolis: Fortress Press.

Lester, Andrew D. (1995). *Hope in Pastoral Care and Counseling*. Louisville: Westminster John Knox Press.

Lewis, C. S. (1961). *A Grief Observed*. New York: The Seabury Press.

Lindemann, Erich (1979). *Beyond Grief: Studies in Crisis Intervention*. Introduction by Bertram S. Brown. London: Jason Aronson.

(Originally published as Lindemann, Erich (1944). "Symptomatology and Management of Acute Grief." *American Journal of Psychiatry* 101: 141–48.)

Lowry, James S. (Easter 1999). "To Preach or Not to Preach: That Is the (Funeral). Question." *Journal for Preachers* 22, no. 3: 39–50.

Mansell, John S. (1998). *The Funeral: A Pastor's Guide.* Nashville: Abingdon Press.

McWilliams, Nancy (1994). *Psychoanalytic Diagnosis: Understanding Personality Structure in the Clinical Process.* New York: The Guilford Press.

Merriam-Webster's Collegiate Dictionary, 10th ed. (1998). Springfield, Mass.: Merriam-Webster.

Mitchell, Kenneth R., and Anderson, Herbert (1983). *All Our Losses, All Our Griefs: Resources For Pastoral Care.* Philadelphia: The Westminster Press.

Moltmann, Jürgen (1996). *The Coming of God: Christian Eschatology.* Translated by Margaret Kohl. Minneapolis: Fortress Press.

The New Westminster Dictionary of Liturgy and Worship (1986). Philadelphia: The Westminster Press.

Noren, Carol M. (2001). *In Times of Crisis and Sorrow: A Minister's Manual Resource Guide.* San Francisco: Jossey-Bass.

Oates, Wayne E. (1955). *Anxiety in Christian Experience.* Philadelphia: The Westminster Press.

—— (1997). *Grief, Transition, and Loss: A Pastor's Practical Guide.* Minneapolis: Fortress Press.

Oxford English Dictionary, 2d ed. (1989). Oxford: Clarendon Press.

Parkes, Colin M. (1972). *Bereavement: Studies of Grief in Adult Life.* Foreword by John Bowlby. New York: International Universities Press.

—— (1987). *Bereavement: Studies of Grief in Adult Life,* 2d ed. Madison, Conn.: International Universities Press.

Pfatteicher, Philip H. (1990). *Commentary on the Lutheran Book of Worship: Lutheran Liturgy in Its Ecumenical Context.* Minneapolis: Augsburg Fortress.

Pincus, Lily (1974). *Death and the Family: The Importance of Mourning.* New York: Pantheon Books.

Presbyterian AIDS Network (1995). *Services of Remembrance: A Worship Resource/Presbyterian AIDS Network.* Louisville: Presbyterian Church (U.S.A.)., Presbyterian AIDS Network.

Presbyterian Church (U.S.A.) (1986). *The Funeral: A Service of Witness to the Resurrection: the Worship of God (Supplemental Liturgical Resource 4).* Philadelphia: The Westminster Press.

—— (1987). *Study Guide to the Funeral: A Service of Witness to the Resurrection (Supplemental Liturgical Resource 4).* Louisville: The Office of Worship of the Presbyterian Church (U.S.A.).

—— (1993). *Book of Common Worship.* Louisville: Westminster/John Knox Press.

Ramshaw, Elaine (1987). *Ritual and Pastoral Care.* Philadelphia: Fortress Press.

Rando, Therese A. (1984). *Grief, Dying, and Death: Clinical Interventions for Caregivers.* Foreword by J. William Worden. Champaign, Ill.: Research Press.

—— (1993). *Treatment of Complicated Mourning.* Champaign, Ill.: Research Press.

Raphael, Beverley (1983). *The Anatomy of Bereavement.* London: Jason Aronson.

Rogers, William (1950). *Ye Shall Be Comforted.* Philadelphia: The Westminster Press.

Setzer, Claudia (March 2001). "Resurrection of the Dead as Symbol and Strategy." In *Journal of the American Academy of Religion* 69, no. 1: 65–101.

Stairs, Jean (2000). *Listening for the Soul: Pastoral Care and Spiritual Direction.* Minneapolis: Fortress Press.

Stephenson, John S. (1994). Grief and Mourning. In *Death & Identity*, 3d ed., edited by R. Fulton and R. Bendiksen. Philadelphia: The Charles Press.

Sullender, Scott R. (1985). *Grief and Growth: Pastoral Resources for Emotional and Spiritual Growth.* New York: Paulist Press.

Switzer, David K. (1970). *The Dynamics of Grief.* Nashville: Abingdon Press.

—— (1974). *The Minister as Crisis Counselor.* Nashville: Abingdon Press.

—— (2000). *Pastoral Care Emergencies.* Minneapolis: Fortress Press. (Originally published as *Pastoral Care Emergencies: Ministering to People in Crisis,* New York: Paulist Press, 1989).

Tillich, Paul (1966). *On the Boundary: An Autobiographical Sketch.* New York: Charles Scribner's Sons.

Turner, Victor (1969). *The Ritual Process: Structure and Anti-Structure.* Ithaca, N.Y.: Cornell University Press.

United Methodist Church (U.S.), (1979). *The Service of Death and Resurrection: The Ministry of the Church at Death, Supplemental Worship Resources 7.* Nashville: Abingdon Press.

—— (1992). *The United Methodist Book of Worship.* Nashville: The United Methodist Publishing House.

Vogel, Linda J. (1996). *Rituals for Resurrection: Celebrating Life and Death.* Nashville: Upper Room Books.

White, James F. (2000). *Introduction to Christian Worship* (3d ed., revised and expanded). Nashville: Abingdon Press.

Willimon, William H. (1979). *Worship as Pastoral Care.* Nashville: Abingdon Press.